CW01642852

PUFFIN BOO

WHAT'S YOUR DREAM?

THE WORKBOOK

CHILDREN'S ILLUSTRATED EDITION

SIMON SQUIBB

WHAT'S YOUR DREAM?

THE WORKBOOK

CHILDREN'S ILLUSTRATED EDITION

SIMON SQUIBB

To Helen Griffiths – the best mum ever and the most loving and supportive wife in the world.

PUFFIN BOOKS

UK | USA | Canada | Ireland | Australia
India | New Zealand | South Africa

Puffin Books is part of the Penguin Random House group of companies whose addresses can be found at global.penguinrandomhouse.com.

www.penguin.co.uk www.puffin.co.uk www.ladybird.co.uk

Penguin Random House UK

What's Your Dream?: Find Your Passion. Love Your Work. Build a Richer Life
published by Century, an imprint of Penguin Random House, in 2025
What's Your Dream?: The Workbook (children's illustrated edition)
published by Puffin Books in 2026

002

Interior design and illustration by Dynamo Ltd.
Printed in Great Britain by Clays Ltd, Elcograf S.p.A.

The authorized representative in the EEA is Penguin Random House Ireland, Morrison Chambers, 32 Nassau Street, Dublin D02 YH68

ISBN: 978–0–241–79814–0

All correspondence to:
Puffin Books
Penguin Random House Children's
One Embassy Gardens, 8 Viaduct Gardens, London SW11 7BW

FSC www.fsc.org MIX Paper | Supporting responsible forestry FSC® C018179

CONTENTS

WHAT'S YOUR NAME?

MY NAME IS

______________________________,

AND I'M

____

YEARS OLD

I wanted to ask you that because, when you write a book, you never know exactly who you are talking to.

Although I could guess, I don't know how tall you are, I don't know if you wear glasses or not, if you prefer football to swimming, or if you prefer jam or Marmite on toast.

There's a lot I don't know about you. But there's also one thing I do know. One thing that I know about you, and about *every single person* who has ever read this book before or is going to read it again.

Something I know *for certain*.

YOU HAVE A DREAM.

A dream. Something you care about and that you *really* want to achieve. A **BIG PLAN** for your life and all the amazing things you want to do in it.

Your dream might be to do something with one of your big passions – like cooking food, playing sport, making music or solving puzzles.

It might be to try and fix a problem you see in the world or to help people.

Or it could be to invent something really cool and original that doesn't exist yet.

Whatever it may be, knowing your dream and trying to

achieve it is one of the *most exciting things* about life. It gives you focus: a goal to work towards. It provides you with purpose: a sense of motivation, that whatever you are doing has a reason behind it.

And that's not all. Do you want to know the best part?

AMAZING THINGS HAPPEN TO PEOPLE WHO DREAM.

Like Serena Williams, one of the most successful tennis players of all time. 'When I was growing up, I had a dream,' she has said. 'My dream was to be the best tennis player in the world.'

Or the actor Tom Holland. He grew up dreaming of Spider-Man. He had Spider-Man on his duvet cover and red-and-blue Spider-Man costumes to dress up in. Aged 13 and already an actor, he said it would be his dream superhero role. At 19 he was cast as Spider-Man and went on to play the part in six massive films. He achieved his dream.

Everyone you admire has a story like this. Everything they have achieved has come from the same place. It began when they were the same age as you. **AND IT STARTED WITH A DREAM.**

That's why I want you to think about your dream. I promise you that you have one, even if you don't know it yet (yes, I can hear you at the back saying, 'Not me, I don't').

I've written this book to help you find the dream within you and to take the first steps towards it.

This is my job: to help people with their dreams. I go around with a microphone asking people what their dream is, then I try to do something to help them achieve it. I might give them money, become the first customer of their business, or post about them on TikTok and Instagram so my audience can discover them.

That's one of the reasons I *know* you have a dream. Because when I ask the question, 'What's your dream?', people aren't always sure. Some say they don't have one. Some know it but are afraid to say it. Others think their dream is impossible to achieve.

But whatever they say, *the dream is there*. Because **EVERYONE** has one. Even if it's buried deep down. Even if that person says that they don't. The dream is always somewhere. It's just waiting for us to find it.

Perhaps you're one of those people who isn't quite sure about their dream yet. Or maybe you're completely certain and can't wait to tell me all about it.

Do you know what your dream is? Circle the number that best describes how you feel:

1 **Yes – I know what my dream is**

2 **Maybe – I have some ideas but I'm not sure**

3 **No – I don't know**

Don't worry if you don't know yet! Whatever answer you have just given, this book is for you. We're going to go on a journey together, looking at why your dream is important, how to discover it, and the steps you can take to turn it into something real.

And we're going to talk about how you can get started on your dream **NOW**. Not waiting until you're older, until you've finished school or have decided what job you want to do. Because you will hear a lot of voices out there telling you that you can't, that you're too young, you don't know enough, and you need money to pursue a dream. I've written this book because I believe those people are wrong. I think you can start making your dream a reality **TODAY**. In fact, I know you can.

This is our job together throughout this book: to discover the dream in you and to put you on the path to achieve it.

There will be lots of help and advice along the way. As examples, I'll share stories of people who have lived their dreams. I'll also ask you (and help to answer) questions that enable you to think more clearly about your dream.

By the end, you will have thought about your dream, written down the first version of it and done lots of things to bring you closer to it.

Because we're not talking here about dreams you wake up from, but a dream you can make come true.

Does that sound good? I'm excited. Let's go!

But first, I've told you a bit about me. Now let's turn things around and talk about you.

WHAT DO YOU LOOK LIKE?

DRAW YOURSELF

Throughout this book there will be exercises like this with space for you to write your ideas. If writing isn't your thing, why not make voice notes instead (you could use a grown-up's phone), or get an adult or older sibling to help you write everything down.

OK, it's time for the next exercise. Pens at the ready!

ONE THING I LIKE TO DO IS . . .

ONE THING I LIKE TO EAT IS . . .

ONE THING I LIKE TO READ ABOUT IS . . .

Chapter 0

GET READY!

When we are going to do something important, what's the first thing we do? We get ready!

If you have an exam, you do your revision first and make sure your pencil case is fully stocked. Before playing a football match, you stretch and warm up. When watching a film, you have the popcorn in your hand before it starts.

That's exactly what we're going to do here: a quick warm-up for the rest of the book. Because we have a LOT of work to do together – thinking about everything that goes into your dream, and all the things you can do to make it happen.

So let's get started with an easy one, a quick exercise to get our minds buzzing and ideas flowing.

It's designed to make you think and answer some questions that may be lurking in the back of your mind.

Because I reckon some of you want to ask:

My response is very simple: **DON'T WAIT**. Don't put off having a dream and trying to pursue it.

Why do I say that? The truth is that the older you get, the harder this becomes. You get weighed down by responsibilities and you start to see the world as other people want you to. You start thinking more about what you *can't do* than what you *want to do.*

I promise you that this is how it happens. And I truly wish I'd known all the things in this book at your age.

My advice to you is start now. Push your limits. Discover how great you can be. And remember that you are only *starting* here. Not conquering the world. Just believing in your dream and taking the first steps towards it. There is plenty of time for everything else. The important thing is to **GET STARTED**. The sooner you do this, the easier the journey will be.

So, what's the exercise? It starts with my son, because when I think about why people your age should pursue their dreams, I think about him. He is 8 years old as I write this, and being his dad has taught me so much. I learn as much from him as he learns from me. There are things he knows much more about than me, and does better than me (one of them, which was a painful lesson, is sword fighting!).

I think that's true about you and your parents, or the adults who look after you, as well. They are learning from you. So have a chat with them and have a think. Then for our first exercise, tell me *three things that you can do better than your grown-ups, and three things your grown-ups can do better than you!*

THREE THINGS THAT I DO BETTER THAN MY GROWN-UPS...

1

2

3

THREE THINGS MY GROWN-UPS DO BETTER THAN ME . . .

1 ....

....

2 ....

....

3 ....

....

Chapter 1

WHY SHOULD I HAVE A DREAM?

I hope you're feeling warmed up now, because we're about to begin for real!

We're going to start with a simple but important question. Why am I asking you to think about your dream? Why is this so important?

We can answer that by looking at a different question, one you are probably familiar with.

I bet you've been asked it before.

WHAT DO YOU WANT TO BE WHEN YOU GROW UP?

Perhaps you have your answer to this question already: you want to be a doctor, teacher, engineer, content creator or footballer.

But whether you know your answer or not, I believe this is the *wrong question*.

I don't believe you should be trying to answer this question *at all.*

Why?

Because the aim of life isn't to 'be' something.

It's to **DO** something.

TO HELP PEOPLE AND MAKE A DIFFERENCE.

I bet if you asked a doctor, they wouldn't say they trained for the job because they liked the title. They would probably say that they became a doctor because they wanted to help people who are ill to get better.

Just like a scientist might say they wanted to discover things and make the world a better place.

And an actor, musician or sports star might say they wanted to entertain people and make them feel happy.

All those people are doing things they are passionate about and love to do – *they are following their dream*. They didn't just want to be in a job, have a title and wear a uniform. They wanted to achieve something.

That's why I don't want you to think about what you're going to *be* when you grow up.

I want you to think about what you're going to *do*. The big goals you want to achieve. The problems you want to solve. The ways you want to help.

That is what having a dream is all about.

IT'S ABOUT FOCUSING ON THE THINGS YOU WANT TO DO WITH YOUR LIFE.

How to turn your passions and interests into something you can do every day. Maybe something which will one day become your career.

Reason #1
for having a dream:

IT ENCOURAGES US TO TAKE ACTION – THINKING ABOUT WHAT WE CAN DO IN OUR LIVES AND HOW WE CAN HELP OTHER PEOPLE.

Perhaps most importantly, it's about how you can use the things you care about to make the lives of other people better too.

Have I convinced you yet? Are you with me on the importance of having a dream?

Just in case you're not, a real-life example may help. Let me introduce you to someone a bit like you, with a big and brilliant dream.

I met Mahi, aged 9, outside my staircase of dreams in London, where people come to press the interactive doorbell and tell me about their dreams.

When I asked Mahi about her dream, I already had an idea what it might be, because she was wearing a red T-shirt with the Ferrari logo on it.

In a clear voice, she told me: **'MY DREAM IS TO BECOME A FORMULA 1 DRIVER WHEN I'M OLDER.'**

Why was this her dream? She loved fast cars, she enjoyed go-karting, and her hero was the F1 champion Lewis Hamilton.

Because Mahi's dream and her confidence were so inspiring, people quickly started to help her.

Lewis Hamilton even saw the video we made about Mahi and sent her his support. One of the top female motor racers in the world, Maya Weug, took Mahi out on the track and gave her tips.

Now Mahi is making content about her F1 passion and training towards her dream of being an F1 professional driver.

I loved Mahi's story and her passion. I think it shows why a dream can be such a powerful thing.

I have met a lot of people in my life, but not many who know what they want as clearly as Mahi did. When I asked her about her dream, she didn't hesitate before telling me. She sounded so confident that I immediately believed her. I knew that Mahi was going to pursue her dream, and that she might one day achieve it.

That is one of the most beautiful things about having a dream. It gives us **A GOAL TO FOCUS ON**. Because of Mahi's dream, she knows exactly what she is working towards. She wakes up every day thinking about what she can do to move one step closer to the dream of being an F1 driver.

Meeting Mahi reminded me of the power of having a dream – a thing we most want to achieve in life. That dream can be a **BIG** dream, and you're never too young to start thinking about yours.

Reason #2 for having a dream:

IT GIVES US FOCUS – A BIG GOAL TO TARGET THAT MEANS WE KNOW EXACTLY WHAT WE WANT TO ACHIEVE.

I liked hearing Mahi's story so much that it helped me realize another of the brilliant things about a dream.

When we have a dream – one of the ones we want to achieve, rather than the kind we wake up from – it gives us something incredibly powerful.

We're not just doing it for ourselves.

Almost always, there is a bigger reason behind it. Something else we are trying to achieve as we follow our dream.

That might be to prove a point, to show other people that something is possible, or to make someone we love feel proud.

We call this having a **PURPOSE**: the reason for your dream and the driving force behind it, like the engine in an F1 car.

This is perhaps my second-favourite word in the English language (you can guess the first, right?).

Your purpose tells you *why* you want to pursue your dream. It makes it feel even more special and important. Although our dream may sometimes feel difficult and far away, our purpose is always close by. It helps to keep us going, because we remember that we are chasing our dream for a good reason.

What was Mahi's purpose?

She didn't just want to become an F1 driver because she likes driving and going fast (although she does!).

Mahi wants to do it because she believes that she can inspire other people along the way. Especially other girls like her.

Because the truth about F1 is it's mainly seen as a sport for boys. Only five women have ever driven in an F1 race, and the last one was all the way back in 1992 (ask your parents how old they were then!).

There's no reason why women can't or shouldn't be F1 drivers. But if most fans are boys, then most people who take up the sport are also going to be boys, and most people who eventually get behind the wheel of an F1 car are going to be men.

Mahi believes it doesn't have to be that way. She thinks girls can drive just as fast as boys, and she wants to prove it. She wants to spread that message while pursuing her own dream, encouraging others to follow in her tracks.

That's her purpose. The reason for her dream.

It means that when Mahi has a bad day, she can remind herself *why* she is doing this, and the reason her dream is so important. Because it's not just about her. It's about every girl who ever thought of driving a racing car but wasn't sure if they could.

That is the power of a dream: it gives us a big **AMBITION** to aim for and helps provide us with **PURPOSE**, the fuel to keep going even when it's difficult.

Reason #3 for having a dream:

IT GIVES US PURPOSE – A POWERFUL REASON FOR PURSUING OUR DREAM THAT KEEPS US ON TRACK TO ACHIEVE IT.

Are you with me yet? Yes? No? Just to make sure, let's have one more example and one more reason why dreams are so important.

I met Stiven when I was filming outside an Underground tube station in East London. He approached me wearing a Colombia football top and a black baseball cap with the New York Yankees logo.

It was the cap that Stiven wanted to talk to me about.

'MY DREAM IS TO HAVE MY OWN HAT BRAND,' he told me.

As we talked some more, I soon learned that this was a dream rooted in far more than fashion.

Stiven told me that three years before, when he was just 12 years old, his mum had surgery that left her struggling to walk. She was raising him as a single parent, which had put a lot of responsibility on him at such a young age.

'It's really difficult for me as well. I'm the man of the house basically,' Stiven said. This helped to inspire his dream, combining his passion with the most important thing in his life.

'I want to have my own brand so I can support my mum.'

I had been talking to Stiven for less than a minute, but already I could see how important this dream was for him. It wasn't just about hats. It was about his family, about supporting his mum and about him stepping up and taking responsibility.

Stiven didn't just have a dream. He also had a powerful **PURPOSE**.

Like Mahi's purpose, this wasn't really about him. It wasn't even limited to his own family. Stiven knew that there were lots of families in situations like his, who were struggling. His purpose was to help them.

This is one of the things that makes having a dream, and a purpose, really powerful. It encourages us to think about how we can **HELP OTHER PEOPLE**. We don't just think about **WHAT** we want to do (the dream), or **WHY** we want to do it (the purpose). We also think about **WHO** we are doing this for.

Most people are doing their job because it allows them to help people in some way.

Doctors and nurses work with people who are very ill because they can help make them better. Farmers go outside to work while it's still dark to ensure we all have food to eat. Police officers put themselves in dangerous situations to try and make other people's lives safer.

This is the secret behind real success. It's not about making money, having fancy titles or a nice big office. It's about using our skills and interests to do something that helps the people around us and makes the world a slightly better place.

This is another thing you get from having a dream: you know **WHO** you want to help, and **HOW**.

Stiven knew exactly who he wanted to help by pursuing his dream: parents like his mum who were having a hard time.

So when I promoted his brand on my social media, and he sold 100 of his hats in just 24 hours, Stiven made a decision. He used some of the money he had made to help his family. But he also made a donation to charity, and he decided to give the rest of the money away to other single mums like his.

Stiven's dream was the hat brand, but his purpose was to support his family and other single-parent families who might also need help.

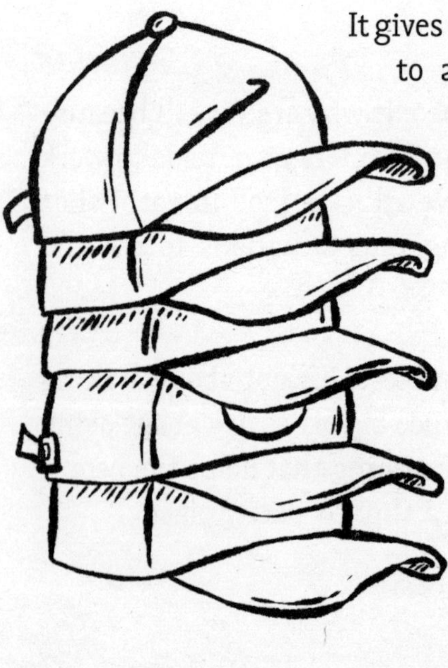

This is the great thing about a dream. It gives us the 'what': the thing we want to achieve. It gives us the 'why': the reason we want to do it. And it gives us the 'who': the people we want to help by doing all this.

Your dream might allow you to help these people directly, by solving a problem they have in their lives.

It might allow you to inspire these people, like Mahi wants to do in the world of F1.

Or it might put you in a position to help these people in other ways, like Stiven is doing.

Whoever these people may be, they are a crucial part of your dream. They make it personal and they make it real.

AND LIFE IS SO MUCH BETTER WHEN WE ARE DOING THINGS WITH AND FOR OTHER PEOPLE – WHEN WE ARE USING OUR SKILLS AND PASSIONS TO HELP OTHERS.

Your dream helps you to think about how to do that.

Reason #4 for having a dream:

IT MAKES US THINK ABOUT WHAT WE CAN DO TO HELP OTHER PEOPLE.

That's quite a lot of information to take in, so let's go back over what we've learned so far.

WHY SHOULD YOU HAVE A DREAM?

To sum it up, I would say this. Anyone in life you admire has a dream, from the celebrities you watch on screen to the best teachers at your school.

They might not call it by that name, but they have a dream – a big and important thing they want to achieve in life. Inside that dream is a purpose, and alongside it is an idea of the people they want to help.

There's a good reason that successful and interesting people tend to have a dream. Because when you have a dream, you gain some very important things with it.

In this chapter, we've looked at four of these:

1. A dream gives you INSPIRATION: the desire to do something rather than to want to 'be' something

2. A dream gives you FOCUS: a goal to keep aiming for and a direction in your life

3. A dream gives you PURPOSE: a deeper sense of motivation, which is important when things get tough

4. A dream gives you a way to show KINDNESS: to help other people as well as yourself

Those are my reasons for why having a dream is extremely useful and pretty cool. But there are lots more, and I'd love you to put them into your own words.

So based on what you have read, and after thinking about it and maybe talking it through with a grown-up or older sibling, try writing out your own! In your own words, say why you think having a dream can be a good thing and how it can be helpful to you and to the other people in your life. Try and give three different reasons.

HAVING A DREAM IS IMPORTANT BECAUSE...

1

....

....

....

2

....

....

....

3

....

....

....

WHO DO I KNOW WHO HAS A DREAM?

WHAT IS THEIR DREAM?

WHAT DREAMS MIGHT MY BEST FRIEND HAVE?

Chapter 2

WHAT'S MY DREAM?

Hopefully by now I've convinced you that having a dream is a really good idea – that it's a great way to pursue the things we love to do, and to help other people while we do it.

If you're with me so far, then the next step is to start thinking about **YOUR** dream!

This is going to take some time and there are a few different steps involved. Your dream is a bit like your favourite pizza or pasta dish: it has several different ingredients and it needs some cooking to make it taste just right.

So even if you are sitting there with a pen in your hand, waiting to tell me exactly what your dream is, I want you to go through these steps with me.

Because if you *don't know* what your dream is yet, this is going to help you find it.

And if you *do know* what your dream is, this is going to help you understand it better.

I'm going to explain how this works by telling you a bit more about my story and my dream.

What's my dream?

MY DREAM IS TO HELP TEN MILLION PEOPLE IN THE WORLD ACHIEVE THEIR DREAMS.

It's a big number, isn't it? In fact, it's a deliberately **HUGE** number, a mountain so tall that I will always have something to aim for however long I am doing this.

How do I try to achieve that dream?

I go out into the world with my microphone and I ask people the same question I am asking you in this book – 'What's your dream?'. Then I see what I can do to help them.

After that I share their stories with the millions of people who follow me on TikTok and Instagram, so that they can help too.

Each person I help and make a video about also **INSPIRES** lots of the people who watch it, who might then think:

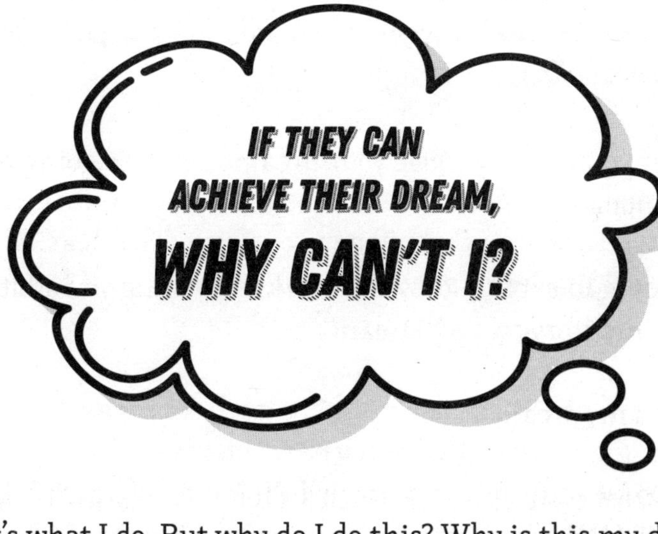

That's what I do. But why do I do this? Why is this my dream, and how did I get there?

The honest answer is I got there very *slowly*. For most of my life (and I'm now over 50, so really old), I didn't think about having a dream. I didn't know why I needed one. That's one of the reasons I've written this book, so you can have the knowledge I didn't when I was your age.

Although it took me a very long time to find my dream, the roots of it began growing when I was quite young.

It was when I was aged 15, probably a little older than you are now. This was when two of the most important events in my life happened. The first was that my dad suddenly died of heart failure. He was there, then suddenly he was gone.

Not long after, my mum and I had a terrible argument. Both of us were so upset about what had happened that we kept falling out. This was the worst row and she told me to get out. I left home and never went back.

Suddenly, my life changed. One day I had been going to school as normal, with a comfortable bed to sleep in, food in the fridge and some pocket money to spend. The next day, all of those things were gone. I was on my own. All I had was a sports bag with my clothes in it.

For a few weeks, I had nowhere to live. I was homeless. Some nights I stayed with friends. On others I was outside. Eventually I found a tiny room in a shared house that was more like a large cupboard. It was somewhere to sleep, but I didn't have any way to pay for it.

I needed to find a way of making money, and I had to do it quickly.

This was when the second turning point happened. I was walking down the street, past a row of beautiful houses, thinking about my own new bedroom and how small it was.

I looked at the houses, with their neat red bricks, white painted window frames, and carefully trimmed green grass at the front.

And I thought:

I'll never be able to live in a house as nice as that.

Then I walked past another of these houses and I **STOPPED**.

Although it was another lovely house that looked like the others, something was different about this one. My eyes had noticed it before my brain caught up. *It was the grass.* It was too long and needed cutting. It was making everything else look untidy.

My brain did some more catching up.

I often think of this as the moment that a switch flicked in my head and I became an entrepreneur – a person who runs their own business rather than working for someone else.

Before I could stop myself, I was ringing the doorbell of that house and asking if they would pay me to cut the grass. The people living there seemed a bit surprised I had asked, but they said yes. I made money doing that job, and soon I was running a gardening business cutting the grass in lots of gardens.

This wasn't my dream, by the way. I didn't dream of being a gardener. I didn't dream of running my own business either: it was just something I had to do to make money and survive.

It would be a long time before I started thinking about dreams and why they matter.

But I was learning things that would eventually lead me to my dream: to help ten million people with *their* dreams.

The first thing I learned is that running a business is hard. Almost everyone who is going to run their own business or pursue their dream **NEEDS HELP**.

The second thing I learned was that help is hard to find. Especially when you don't have the money to pay for it. I remember asking one local business owner for advice. He wanted me to pay for his help, but I said I couldn't. I've never forgotten his response. **'IF YOU DON'T PAY, YOU DON'T PAY ATTENTION.'**

I couldn't pay, so I didn't get help.

Many years later, after I had run a lot more businesses and made quite a lot of money, I thought back to that conversation.

For the first time, I started to think about my dream.

I knew that a lot of people wanted to run their own business, *but they didn't know how.* Just like me at 15, they needed help. And they needed that help for free.

Now I was in a position to provide people with that help – the kind of help I couldn't get when I had really needed it.

That's how I discovered my dream to help ten million people with their dreams.

It was by putting together ingredients, like a recipe:

- Something I was PASSIONATE about: helping people with their businesses and listening to their dreams.
- Something I had the POTENTIAL to do: I had learned a lot about how to run a business by this point, and had lots of knowledge to share.
- Something that was PERSONAL to me: it reminded me of when I was young, had tried to get help and hadn't been able to find it.

I believe every dream combines these three things. That's why I don't want you to jump to the end and tell me your dream straight away.

I want us to start with the things that go into it, working out what your secret ingredients are before we mix them together.

Just like a pizza comes out of the oven with the crust perfectly golden and the cheese beautifully melted, your dream is going to be so much better for the time we spend cooking it. So, let's get started and gather our ingredients.

INGREDIENT #1: PASSION

Passion is the most obvious and also the most important part of a dream.

A dream has to start with *you*: the things you love to do, the things you care about, the things you spend all your spare time and pocket money on.

We all have passions, and the best thing is that they are ours.

Other people might not understand them, they might even laugh at them (which is their problem), but **WE** know why these things are interesting and important.

Do you know the coolest thing about your passions?

YOU CAN MAKE A DREAM OUT OF THEM!

You can share the things you love with other people, find other people who have the same interests, and maybe even turn it into a way to make money.

Whether you love music, netball, rock climbing, reading, cooking, Minecraft or Fortnite, there are so many things you can do to turn a passion into a dream.

Let's look at how that works with a few examples.

Maybe you love climbing, you go for a lesson every week and it's one of your favourite things to do.

How does that become a dream? There are lots of different ways. Your dream could be to go rock climbing in some of the coolest and most challenging places in the world. It could be to inspire other people to share the sport you love by becoming a trainer. It could be to change the way people think about climbing by designing new clothing or equipment.

Or maybe music is your thing. People your age and a bit older tell me *all the time* about their big dreams in music. Some of them want to be in famous bands. Others want to become DJs and share their taste in music with big crowds. Another way could be to become a content creator, sharing your views on music.

Then there's cooking. This is another popular one. Your dream might be to work as a chef in a restaurant one day. It could be to have your own shop selling cakes and sweet treats. It might be to create your own recipes and become a culinary influencer or a recipe-book writer.

Now, your dream might not be any of these things. It might not even be **CLOSE** to any of the things I have just mentioned.

But I hope you will see what I'm trying to show you here. That a dream starts with a **PASSION**, something you love to do and care about. And that passion can lead you in **LOTS OF DIFFERENT DIRECTIONS**, enabling you to do all sorts of amazing things.

There are loads of ways to turn your passions into dreams.

YOU CAN CHOOSE YOUR OWN ADVENTURE, AND THAT'S WHAT MAKES IT SO FUN.

As you do that, please try and remember these two things:

1 **Your dream starts with something you love, which is personal to you, and which you are completely fascinated by. You can't borrow your dream from someone else, and you shouldn't do it because you think it sounds cool. It should be based on something you actually love to do.**

2 **You don't have to be 'the best' at something to build your dream around it. Not many of us get to be chart-topping singers or Premier League footballers. That doesn't mean we can't have dreams about music or sport. There are so many ways to turn a passion into a dream. Everyone has passions, and everyone should have a dream.**

Thinking about all of that, let's talk about your passions and do a quick exercise. Write a sentence or two about the thing you most love to do in your spare time and tell me a little about why.

Then, thinking about the examples above, tell me **ONE WAY** that you could turn that passion into a dream.

WHAT'S MY BIGGEST PASSION IN LIFE – THE THING I MOST ENJOY DOING?

....

....

....

WHAT'S ONE WAY I COULD TURN THIS INTO A DREAM?

(THIS DOESN'T HAVE TO BE YOUR DREAM FOR REAL – WE'RE JUST BRAINSTORMING HERE!)

....

....

....

....

INGREDIENT #2: POTENTIAL

After passion comes potential. As we start thinking about how to turn the things we like doing into dreams, we need to focus on our abilities – the things we are really good at.

What do I mean by this?

If you think about the passion you have just written about, I reckon you could tell me the thing you like **MOST** about it. The bit of it you're really good at doing. The thing that gives you the most joy.

Like whether you prefer listening to music or making your own music.

If you're better at talking about your favourite games or playing them.

If you like designing things on the computer in a DT lesson or making them with your hands.

Thinking more about your passion, tell me the specific bit of it that you really love – the thing you most like to do:

____

____

____

Whatever your passion may be, it's probably quite a broad one. Lots of people share it, and they all have their reasons for loving it. But **YOUR** version of that passion is special.

No one else thinks about this thing the way you do, or enjoys it in exactly the same way.

That is how we discover our potential: the thing we have a **SPECIAL ABILITY** to do.

We start with a thing we love to do.

Then we dig a little deeper.

WHY DO I REALLY LIKE THIS?

....

....

WHY DOES IT MAKE ME FEEL GOOD?

....

....

HOW DOES IT ALLOW ME TO USE MY SKILLS AND TALENTS AS A PERSON?

....

....

....

Let's look at a few examples I often hear from people your age.

Some dreamers tell me they really want to start their own clothing brand. Their passion is clothes and fashion. Their special skill is that they really enjoy making their own designs. So their potential is to one day become someone who designs clothes for a major label, or creates their own!

Passion + special skill = potential

Perhaps you absolutely love animals: that's your passion. And maybe you're very good at keeping them calm, like when your dog needs to take some medicine. That's your special skill. So your potential might be to work as a vet or animal trainer, combining your passion for pets with your ability to take care of them.

Or maybe your favourite thing is running. And although you can run pretty fast, your special skill is encouraging others to complete the course after you, cheering and helping them on. Your potential could be to become a running coach, to start your own running club or to create content encouraging people to take up running for the first time.

That's how we take a passion and discover what it allows us to do – our potential.

Now it's your turn, and time for another exercise. You're going to write down three things: your passion, the part of it you're **REALLY GOOD AT**, and then your potential – the thing you can do as a result.

MY PASSION IS . . .

(HINT: YOU ALREADY ANSWERED THIS!)

MY SPECIAL SKILL (THE BIT OF THIS I'M REALLY GOOD AT) IS . . .

MY POTENTIAL (THE THING I CAN DO COMBINING THAT SKILL WITH THAT PASSION) IS . . .

INGREDIENT #3: SOMETHING PERSONAL

Now for the third ingredient in our recipe of dreams. This is the last one – maybe the most important one.

I'm calling it **SOMETHING PERSONAL**.

Wait a minute, you might be thinking. *We already talked about my passion, and that's personal. And my potential: that's pretty personal too.* And you're right!

But we don't just have one passion in life. We have the potential to do lots of different things.

So it's this third ingredient – the something personal – that helps us to make sure we are actually cooking up a dream here.

What am I talking about?

By something personal, I mean something that is **UNIQUE** to you. A thing that happened in your life, which is important in a way only you can fully understand.

Maybe it was your grandma who taught you to bake cakes, and now you want to share some of her recipes and her love with other people.

Maybe you had a difficult experience in your life, like being ill or getting bullied, and now you want to help other children who are going through the same things.

Perhaps you were told that you weren't good enough to play football, or you weren't tall enough to play basketball, and you want to prove that person wrong.

These are personal experiences that play a huge role in forming our dreams.

Having a passion and working out your potential are important.

But often the true motivation, the thing that makes you *really* want to do this, comes from something personal.

When I talk to people about their dreams, there is almost always a deeply personal reason behind them.

We all have these experiences, and they can happen early in our lives.

One of my first came when I was the same age as you, in school. I am dyslexic, which means I mix my words up and find it difficult to read. Today this is a well-understood condition and people get help with it. If you are dyslexic, it means you see the world in a different way, and there are advantages to this as well as problems to overcome.

But when I was at school, dyslexia wasn't properly understood, so people just thought you must be stupid.

Other kids in my class would laugh when I tried to read something out and got the words wrong. I think some of the teachers made a point of asking me to read because they knew I found it difficult. It felt like they were laughing at me as well.

That experience showed me that we all learn in different ways – we all need different kinds of help to succeed. That's one of the big reasons I like helping people with their dreams. Often people have amazing ideas and talents, but school hasn't given them the right support. It's one of the reasons I'm writing this book!

The second experience was when I was kicked out of home at 15 and had to start my own business, as I told you about earlier.

That was such a hard thing to do and I made loads of mistakes. I wish that I'd had help then. So the idea that people need help with their dreams – like I did at 15 – is also something personal to me. I try to help as many people as possible, and to encourage others to provide help, *because I remember how hard it was for me.*

That's what I mean by having something personal — a motivation that comes from your life experiences, often some kind of pain or adversity. It makes the dream more authentic, and it makes it stronger too.

Now it's time to focus on your 'something personal'. Think about an experience in your life that helps to explain **WHY** you care about the passion and potential you've already written down.

WHAT WAS AN IMPORTANT PERSONAL EXPERIENCE IN MY LIFE?

....

....

....

HOW DOES THAT EXPERIENCE LINK TO MY PASSION? WHAT HAS IT MADE ME CARE ABOUT?

....

....

....

WHAT DO I WANT TO DO AS A RESULT?

....

....

....

Chapter 3

OK, BUT WHAT'S MY DREAM?

At this point we've done a lot of important work.

You've thought about the things you are passionate about in life, your special skills and abilities, and why these things are important to you.

That's a great start: lots of grown-ups have never properly thought about these things at all!

THESE ARE THE THINGS THAT DREAMS ARE MADE OF.

Now, I can almost hear some of you saying: What about my dream? What is it? How do I find it? How do I put it into words?

Well, like a chef, we have to combine the ingredients we have just prepared.

The way I like to think about it is this:

Your **PASSION** points you towards the dream. You know it's going to be something related to this, because it can't be a dream unless you really care about it.

Your **POTENTIAL** helps to narrow it down, focusing on the bit of your passion that you are really good at or interested in.

And your **SOMETHING PERSONAL** helps to ensure that the dream is rooted in a thing that is unique to you.

How do we connect all of these pieces to find our dream?

A bit like a difficult maths problem, sometimes it's helpful to look at the answer and work backwards from there.

Let's look at a few examples of people around your age who have found their dreams, and how they did it. Then we'll use those to look at how you can find *your* dream.

These are all people I have met in the course of making videos and helping people with their dreams.

One really inspiring dreamer was Freya, aged 8, whose dream was to be a famous YouTuber.

Let's break down the ingredients of her dream.

Freya's **PASSION** was that she loved animals and talking about them. If you watch our video together, you will see we went to a farm to film her first video.

Her **POTENTIAL** was that she had a wonderfully clear voice and an infectiously positive personality. She is exactly the kind of person who comes across well on camera and who people want to listen to.

Freya also had **SOMETHING PERSONAL** that held her dream together. As she told me: 'I was poorly. When I was one or two years old, I had cancer. I was close to dying. So I can entertain the world, and when I get money I can give it to charities.'

That is an inspiring dream with an incredible purpose. It also shows **EXACTLY HOW** a dream brings together the three main ingredients we've talked about.

At first, the dream to be a content creator sounds like something that anyone could have.

But as Freya explained, that dream was special to her. Because of the terrible time she'd had with illness, she wanted to help other people who were going through the same thing. The way she planned to do that was to turn her *passion* for animals and her *potential* as a presenter into content creation. She would use this to raise money and donate it to charities that helped young people with cancer – that was her *purpose*.

It's a beautiful example of how a dream, the thing we want to achieve, contains a passion, the thing we love to do, and is driven by a purpose, the reason why we are doing it.

Now let's look at another story.

Not long after filming with Freya, I met Raees, who was 14. He told me, **'MY DREAM IS TO OWN A BUSINESS.'**

He knew exactly what kind of business it would be. Raees liked fashion, but his parents didn't have much spare money to spend. He knew how much the clothes he liked cost, and that they were too expensive for families like his.

His dream business planned to change that. He wanted to buy branded clothing second-hand, make it look as good as new, and then sell it at a price that more people could afford to buy.

This is another dream with a strong passion, based on skills and knowledge, and rooted in personal life experience.

But what were they?

Based on what I've said, I want *you* to tell *me* what you think the ingredients of Raees's dream are. If it helps, you can go on my TikTok or Instagram (with a grown-up's help) and find the video I filmed with him. Once you've had a look and a think, then have a go at filling out the questions opposite, just like I did with Freya's story earlier. If you're struggling, read back what I have written about Raees: all the clues are there.

Remember, we're doing this because once you look at someone else's dream and work out how it came together, it will be so much easier to discover your own dream. It means you understand what a dream is and what it contains.

I THINK RAEES'S PASSION IS . . .

I THINK RAEES'S POTENTIAL IS . . .

I THINK RAEES'S SOMETHING PERSONAL IS . . .

I've told you Raees's and Freya's stories because we can learn a lot about our dreams from other people. Although your dream is unique to you, the idea of having a dream is not. I wanted you to see exactly how people similar in age to you have taken their passions, their potential and their personal life experiences, and made them into dreams.

Learning from others is great. But ultimately we're talking about *your* dream. And that's exactly what we're going to do next.

As we work out your dream, I want you to remember one thing.

The dream might be small or it could be massive, *and it really doesn't matter.*

If you want to climb Everest and conquer the world before you've sat your GCSEs, then I don't want to discourage you. People your age and younger have achieved **AMAZING** things.

Children have composed symphonies, been recruited to NASA and become champion chess players, all by the age of 12.

But I also don't want you to think that your dream *has* to be something big and scary. Little dreams are important too. Achieving them will mean that when we're older and want to tackle something more ambitious, we're ready.

So although you can learn from other people's dreams, don't be influenced by them. Don't worry if someone else's dream sounds bigger and better than yours. A small dream that you achieve is better than a huge one that you give up on after a week. The most important thing is that the dream feels **RIGHT FOR YOU.**

OK, let's get down to it and build your dream.

The method I'm going to share with you is simple. You take all the things we've worked on so far and you connect them together. Put another way, you make a story out of them.

One of the most important words in any story is the word *because*.

Both in real life and in fiction, things happen *because* people made a certain choice.

You're reading this book *because* you saw one of my videos online, or *because* one of your friends recommended it, or *because* you saw the cover and liked it. (Or maybe for some other reason, but it's definitely because of *something*!)

I wrote this book *because* I want more people like you to chase their dreams. And in a deeper sense, *because* I was once young, needed help and couldn't get it, and I never want anyone else to be in the same position that I was.

Now we are going to apply the 'because' method to working out your dream.

It goes like this:

***BECAUSE** I have a passion in life, something I love to do . . .*

***AND BECAUSE** that passion is linked to something I do well (my potential) or something personal that happened in my life . . .*

***THEREFORE** my dream is . . .*

Let's go back to Freya's story to see how this works.

STEP 1:
Name your passion

STEP 2:
link it to your personal experience or potential (or both!)

STEP 3:
Name your dream!

STEP 4:
Say what your dream will allow you to do (this is your purpose)

BECAUSE FREYA'S PASSION IS . . .
Sharing her love for animals

AND BECAUSE HER PERSONAL EXPERIENCE IS . . .
Overcoming cancer as a very young child

FREYA'S DREAM IS . . .
To become a content creator

SO THAT SHE CAN . . .
Raise money for charities helping children with cancer

You'll notice that I snuck in an extra box at the end. Remember earlier when we talked about purpose and helping other people? How Stiven wanted to help single parents with his hat company, and how Mahi wanted to inspire other girls to get involved with F1?

That's the fourth box. The purpose. The reason why we do the dream, and the other people we are doing it for.

OK, now it's your turn. The big moment. It's time to put a name on your dream. Take your time and have a go at filling out the answers yourself, starting from the top. Remember, we've already been through some of these, so now your focus is fitting it all together and thinking about what goes in the crucial third section.

This is one of the most important exercises in the book, so don't rush it!

BECAUSE MY PASSION IS . . .

....

....

AND BECAUSE MY PERSONAL EXPERIENCE OR POTENTIAL IS . . .

....

....

MY DREAM IS TO...

....

....

....

SO THAT I CAN . . .

....

....

You've done it! You've named your dream. It might only be one sentence, but I can promise you that this is a massively important step. In fact, it's a step that lots of people never take. **A MASSIVE WELL DONE FOR GETTING THIS FAR**.

Take a pause for breath and then let's carry on. Because by answering one big question, we have earned ourselves another.

Is this **REALLY** my dream?

A lot of people get to this point and ask themselves this. They wonder if they've got it right. They worry they might be barking up the wrong tree completely.

So how can you be sure? Is that even possible?

I have two things to say about this. The first is don't worry too much about it. You are young and it's very possible that a year from now, and certainly in five or ten years, your dream will have changed. You will have seen more of the world, had more experiences, and know for sure what you want to dedicate your life to.

So don't stress about whether your passions might change in the future and make this dream something that no longer feels so important for you. If and when that happens, you will still be grateful that you had a dream and you chased it. You will learn so much from understanding and trying to achieve your dream **RIGHT NOW**. That's the only thing I want you to focus on. Let your future self worry about the future.

But what about that present dream? Are you sure you've got it right?

No one can ever be certain, but there is a little test you can do.

It's incredibly easy and it works like this. **YOU DO NOTHING.** You carry on with your life as normal, for a few days or maybe a week. And you wait.

The test is: are you thinking about your dream?

When you're trying to fall asleep at night, is it on your mind?

When you're bored during a car journey, do you start going over it in your head?

When you have some free time, are you researching what you need to do to get started?

IF ANY OF THOSE THINGS DESCRIBE YOU, THEN CONGRATULATIONS. IT'S DEFINITELY YOUR DREAM.

But if a week has gone by since you've filled out those boxes and you haven't thought about your dream once, then you might need to have another go.

This test works because a real dream is something that is so important to us that *we can't stop thinking about it.* We don't forget it exists. It's there in the bit of our brain that works away in the background, nagging away, asking questions, prodding you to do something.

If none of that is happening, then go back to the boxes and look again at your answers. You're probably pretty close, but like a chair that's wobbling, one or two of the screws need to be tightened up.

Maybe you've got the passion right but you haven't been specific enough about either your potential or personal experience. You haven't narrowed down that passion to the bit you are really good at, or shown how it links to the thing that happened in your life which motivates you.

Or perhaps you need to work on the purpose, linking your dream to the thing it will help you to achieve, just like how Freya wants to use her YouTube channel to raise money for charities, or Raees wants more people to get joy out of fashion.

Keep playing around until you've got the combination right and you've named a dream that you are thinking about every day. At that point, you *know* it's right. The dream will lodge in your brain and it will keep nagging you until you start doing something about it.

Which leads us to the next stage. Now you have the dream in place, how can you start making it a reality?

Chapter 4

I'M READY! HOW DO I GET STARTED?

BEGINNINGS CAN BE SCARY

We all know what it feels like to walk into a new classroom or group situation for the first time when we don't know anyone. Will we like people? Will they like us? Will we make friends?

That's how most people feel when trying something new for the first time. We're unsure because we haven't done it before. We're worried about getting something wrong or embarrassing ourselves.

It's no different when it comes to your dream.

Whatever it is, it's going to take you into unfamiliar territory. Having a passion for fashion, cooking or gaming is one thing, but it doesn't mean you know how to design your own clothes, sell your own food or successfully host a stream.

Actually making a start on your dream can be scary – I get it. But this is a good thing! A big part of life is doing things that we find intimidating and overcoming that fear. Usually, once we've actually *done* the thing we were worrying about, we realize it wasn't as hard as we thought. Then we're ready to do it again. We *want* to do it again.

Your dream is going to make you try new things and push yourself. Even if it will sometimes seem difficult, I guarantee that you will feel *amazing* when you achieve the things you were afraid of doing.

→ SO HOW *DO* YOU GET STARTED WITH YOUR DREAM?

This is a question I get asked all the time by people your age and much older. Some people already know their dream (the same stage you've now reached). Their problem is that they don't know what to do. They can't work out their first step. *They're stuck.*

A lot of people in this situation have the same problem. They are making the dream *more complicated than it needs to be.* They are thinking one hundred steps ahead rather than just one. They try to work out **EVERYTHING** they will need to achieve their dream, and it starts to scare them. They think it's too much, that they don't know enough, or that they need money to get started.

It's a good example of how we put obstacles in our own way.

When it comes to getting started with a dream, often the biggest barrier is **US**.

We are the ones saying that it might be too hard, that we're not ready, or that we may fail. When I go around asking people about their dreams, the **NUMBER ONE** thing people say to me is that they have a dream but they're afraid to do it. They're more worried about what could go wrong than they are excited about achieving their dreams.

THERE'S ONLY ONE WAY TO OVERCOME THIS.
WE **HAVE TO TAKE RESPONSIBILITY FOR GETTING STARTED, PUTTING OUR FEARS TO ONE SIDE SO WE CAN TAKE ACTION. EACH PERSON HAS TO DO THIS FOR THEMSELF – NO ONE ELSE CAN DO IT FOR YOU.**

I learned this lesson when I was 15. I saw the long grass in someone's garden and thought I could make money by becoming a gardener.

If I'd taken too long to think about it, I might have let the doubts pile up around me. I'd never done any proper gardening before, so I wasn't qualified. I didn't own any equipment. I didn't have anyone to recommend me or say that I could do a good job.

There were lots of good reasons for me **NOT** to ring on the doorbell of that first house and ask if I could work on their garden. In fact, there were more reasons against it than for it.

This is going to happen when you try to start working on your dream. The rational bit of your brain will be telling you to stop. It will say that the time is not right, you're not ready, and what if it all goes wrong?

This is what we call overthinking. If you spend too much time thinking about **ANYTHING**, then you will start to doubt yourself. There is always a reason not to do something if you look hard enough for it.

The antidote to overthinking is to trust your instincts. This is your dream and it's important to you. *It's better to try and risk failure than to not try at all.*

It's also true that you should start to take action **QUICKLY**. Don't let your dream hang around until after Christmas or through the long summer holiday. I promise that the longer you wait, the harder it's going to be to get started. Doubts grow larger the longer we let them rattle around in our heads. The way to get rid of them is to start *doing* things and prove to ourselves that our fears weren't real.

I think you probably know this already. Even better, we can prove it. Time for a quick exercise. I want you to tell me something that you used to be afraid of or worry about, but that you're not any more. Then tell me what helped you to overcome that fear.

SOMETHING I USED TO WORRY ABOUT IS . . .

I NO LONGER WORRY ABOUT IT BECAUSE . . .

TAKE THE FIRST STEP

Now you've reminded yourself that you can overcome your fears, let's get started with your dream.

At this point I want you to focus on two very important words: *first step*.

Whatever your dream is, there are going to be lots of steps involved. That dream might feel very far away, and it could take you months or even years of work to get there.

If you want to build an audience for your YouTube channel, find people to join a club you've started or get customers for your business, then that won't happen quickly. No success happens overnight or by magic. Sometimes people online or celebrities might make it look easy, but I promise you it isn't.

I need you to understand that, and then to forget about it for a moment. I don't want you to worry about all those steps for now. I don't want you to try and plan everything out in advance. **I JUST WANT YOU TO TAKE THE FIRST STEP.**

Why? Because if you try to map everything out at the beginning, you will probably never start at all. It's going to feel like too much. That's why skydivers aren't supposed to look down before jumping out of a plane, because it makes them realize how far they have to fall. The more time we have to think about something, the harder it becomes to take action.

My advice at this point is: don't think about all the things you are going to have to do to make your dream come true.

Narrow it down to **ONE THING** that is the best way to get started.

The only rule is that this thing has to be something real. A proper step towards your dream, not a pretend one.

I think you know what I mean by this.

It's a bit like when you're revising for an exam. You organize your pencil case, you make notes, you organize those notes, and time passes. You feel busy.

But what did you really achieve? Not very much! Because you weren't really revising, you were finding things to do instead of revise. You were putting the hard part off because you didn't really want to do it.

Everyone does this sometimes, including grown-ups. That's OK, but it's a problem when the pretend work takes the place of real work.

So the first step towards your dream isn't sharpening your pencil, making a list or colour-coding your ideas. It's something real that takes you a step **CLOSER** to actually achieving the dream.

That *doesn't* mean the first step has to be big or difficult. It might be something that only takes a few minutes.

The test for whether this step is useful or not is that it should leave you with something you didn't already have. And this should help you with your dream.

If your dream is to launch some kind of clothing brand, then your first step could be to make one of the customized hats, pairs of shoes or T-shirts that you are thinking of. Or it might be to sketch a design that someone else can help you to make. Then you have a **PRODUCT** – something you can show to people and potentially sell.

If the dream is to become a content creator, then a good first step would be to set up your social media channels and record your first video. Then you have some **CONTENT** to promote.

If your dream is to be a singer or skateboarder, then your first step could be to record yourself performing. Then you have some **EVIDENCE** of your talent that you can share.

Or if your dream is to run a tech company, or create a new app, then your first step could be to learn to code something using one of the AI tools that now make this much easier than before. Then you have developed a **SKILL** that you can use to build the app you think needs to exist.

Those are just some examples. Let's work out what *your* first step is going to be.

A few hints:

It should be something you can start doing right now, maybe with a little help from a sibling or a grown-up.

It should be something that brings you closer to your dream, even in a small way. This isn't about preparation but **ACTION**.

It should be something you can do quite quickly, so you can see the results and know that you've made progress.

Have a think about all of that and then write down what your first step is going to be. You'll notice I'm also asking you to write down your dream again. This isn't a misprint: it's important to keep talking about the dream, to say it and note it down. This helps to remind us why we're doing all of this! If you're the kind of person who likes to make notes and lists, then make sure to write your dream on all of them. Keep reinforcing what you are trying to achieve.

MY DREAM IS . . .

....

....

....

AS THE FIRST STEP TOWARDS MY DREAM, I WILL . . .

....

....

....

Once you've done that exercise, then I want you to **STOP READING**.

That's an unusual thing for the author of a book to say. Usually we want you to keep reading!

But I really want you to **STOP** and put the book down (just for now). Can you guess why?

I want you to take that first step!

Go and do the thing you said you would do. Set up the social accounts, record the content, design the product or write the recipe.

Only after you've done this do I want you to pick up the book again and read the next bit. I trust you. Good luck!

WHAT NOW?

If you've reached this point, well done!

Not only have you named your dream but you've taken an important step towards it.

In fact, it's *the* most important step. The first one is the hardest. Before this you were standing on the diving board, thinking about how high it was, wondering if the water was cold and if it might sting.

You were thinking about your dream, and now you've started doing it. That is massive!

How does it feel? I bet you're a bit more confident now than you were before. That the dream is starting to seem a bit more real. I'd love you to tell me about it.

AS THE FIRST STEP TOWARDS MY DREAM, I HAVE JUST . . .

....

....

....

AS A RESULT, I FEEL . . .

....

....

....

That is the advantage of taking action. It doesn't matter if you took a small step or a big one. Because once you start moving, it is so much easier to keep going. You're walking downhill now, not uphill.

You've proven to yourself that you can do something. And your brain starts to think: *OK, what's next?*

Let's think about it.

I'm pretty sure that your first step was about the 'what' of your dream – the thing you are trying to achieve. You created a design, you filmed a video or you set up your profiles online.

And that's great. But dreams are about 'who' as well as 'what'. You need other people in your dream: the people you are trying to sell your clothes or cakes to, the people you are trying to entertain through music or content, the people who can spot your talent as a guitar player or athlete.

So your next step is to work out **WHO** you can get to help you with your dream.

This is a really important step, because your dream doesn't really start to happen *until you get other people involved.*

If you want to become a singer, then you will need to approach the person who runs the choir at school (or in your local area) and ask for an audition.

If you want someone like me to help promote your channel, then you need to ask them.

And if you want someone to buy the thing you are making, then you need to sell it to them.

Remember one of the first things we discussed in this book: other people are fundamental to every dream.

- If you want to be a musician, an athlete or any other kind of entertainer, then that relies on other people watching and enjoying it.
- If you want to run a business of any description, it relies on other people buying the thing you are selling.
- If you want to be a competitive gamer, then you need other people to play against and to be part of your audience.
- Even if you want to do something that sounds completely individual, like climbing the highest mountain in the world on your own, you're not really going to do that alone. You'll need people to teach you, to recommend the right equipment and to help guide you on the climb itself.

Whatever your dream is, I guarantee that it will **DEPEND ON OTHER PEOPLE** to achieve it.

Those people aren't telepathic. They don't know what your dream is unless you tell them. They can't help you unless you ask for it.

So you have to work out *who* can help you with your dream, and *how* you can get their help.

There are two parts to this.

The first is what sort of people *in general* can help you with your dream.

- If you're making content about football, then that means football fans who spend time online.
- If you're trying to work with animals, it's probably the people running vets, pet shops and animal shelters in your local area.
- If you're trying to start a clothing label, then it's probably other kids your age who might share your fashion sense, or people who work either making or selling clothes (maybe start with the owner of your local clothes shop?).

That helps you to narrow it down, because there are some things that could be a waste of your time, like trying to get your grandma to watch a gaming stream. You need to be targeting the right audience – other people who are interested in the same things as you are, who might become your subscribers, customers or supporters.

Have a think and then try to answer my question below. If you can, write down two or three different answers.

THE PEOPLE WHO CAN HELP ME WITH MY DREAM (IN GENERAL) ARE . . .

That's a good start, but now you need to get *specific.*

Because you can't target everyone all at once. You have to start with one or two people. If they like what you're doing, then they might mention it to a friend. That's how two becomes three, three turns into six, which grows into twelve, and so on.

Again, we're thinking one step at a time. Not trying to build a massive audience in one go, but to find a few people who will be interested in your dream and agree to help you.

- They might help you by promoting or subscribing to your social media channel (I do this for dreamers I meet all the time).
- They might become your first customer, buying the T-shirt you've made or the cake you've baked.
- They might give the opportunity to get experience that's relevant to your dream.
- These might be people you already know, like other kids at your school or your next-door neighbours.
- They might be people you know *about*, like social media influencers whose work is related to your dream.
- Or they might be people you don't know at all, but who have knowledge they can share and advice they can give.

Important note:
Before contacting anyone you don't already know well, you need to get permission and help from your parents or a responsible caregiver.

We're now going to make a list of these specific people. I want you to think of **THREE** names.

Why three? Because not everyone will agree to help us with our dreams. If you pin all your hopes on one person and they say no, it can be deflating. But if you carefully pick three people you can approach for help in some way, there's a good chance that at least one of them will say yes.

So have a think of your three people (this is definitely one I want you to discuss with your grown-ups). Then write down the three names, what they can do to help you with the dream, and how you are going to ask them for help. Think about whether it's someone you know and who you can ask in person, or if it's someone you might have to DM (with the help of a grown-up).

THE ***FIRST*** PERSON WHO COULD HELP
ME WITH MY DREAM IS . . .

....

THE WAY THEY COULD HELP
ME WITH MY DREAM IS . . .

....

....

I COULD ASK FOR THEIR HELP BY . . .

....

....

THE ***SECOND*** PERSON WHO COULD HELP
ME WITH MY DREAM IS . . .

....

THE WAY THEY COULD HELP
ME WITH MY DREAM IS . . .

....

....

I COULD ASK FOR THEIR HELP BY . . .

THE ***THIRD*** PERSON WHO COULD HELP ME WITH MY DREAM IS . . .

THE WAY THEY COULD HELP ME WITH MY DREAM IS . . .

I COULD ASK FOR THEIR HELP BY . . .

The list you've just made is really important. The people on it will be crucial to making progress with your dream.

Now you have to get their help. This is another thing that can feel scary: to ask someone if they will help you, listen to you or consider buying something from you.

But you have a **BIG** advantage when doing this.

You have a dream, and that dream contains a purpose.

I promise you this makes it *much easier* to ask for people's help and to get them to listen to you.

I know this because my entire life now is about helping people and being asked for help. I have learned that the people I can help most are the people who are very clear about their dream and purpose.

A good example is Snaffle, aged 12, who told me his dream was to open a restaurant so that he could help to feed the homeless. Within that dream was another purpose, which was to help pay for his parents to retire so he could spend more time with them.

When I hear a dream like that, I immediately start thinking of ways I can help. I *really want* to help because I'm inspired by what I have heard and I want to do my bit to make it happen.

The same applies to a lot of the young people I have talked about so far.

To Freya, who wants to create content so she can raise money for cancer charities.

To Stiven, who wants to help single parents by selling hats.

To Raees, who wants to help more families afford designer clothes through his business.

Because their dreams are clear and their purpose is powerful, people help them.

That's why I don't think you should be scared about asking people for help. By this point you know what your dream and your purpose are. You know what you want to do and *why* you are doing it. If you can communicate that to the people you have listed above, I believe at least some of them will help you.

That's your next challenge. Work out the help you need, work out who can help you, and go and ask for it! Take your dream to the next stage by getting other people on board. This is when it really starts to feel real.

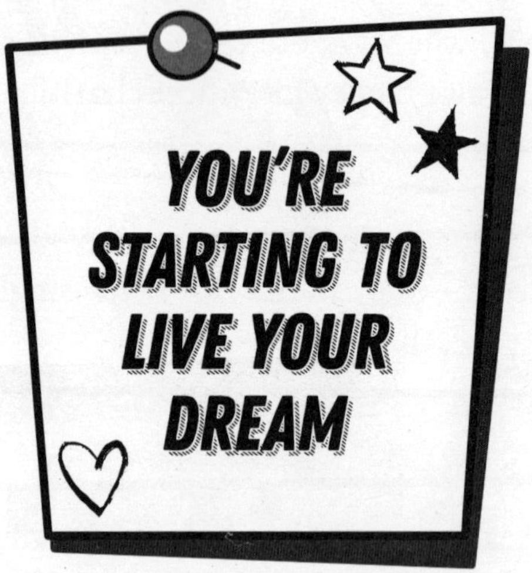

Chapter 5

I'VE STARTED! WHAT NOW?

We're now about halfway through our journey together, so let's recap.

- You've discovered your dream, thinking deeply about the things that matter to you, the things you're good at and the experiences you've had in life.
- You've made a crucial first step towards that dream by taking one concrete action.
- You've thought about the people who can help you with your dream, and how you can get that help.

Hopefully you're now raring to go, full of ideas about what to do next!

But I understand that this can be a difficult point in the journey as well. Once you're walking the path towards your dream, you start to think about how far away it is.

You've taken one step and realize: *wow, there's a lot further to go! This isn't going to be easy.*

The challenge now is to keep going. To build on the momentum you have created by taking the first step. To make sure that you are constantly moving **FORWARD** towards your dream.

HOW CAN WE DO THAT?

In this chapter I'm going to take you through two key parts of this:

HOW TO FIND A **METHOD** FOR WHAT YOU DO THAT ALLOWS YOU TO KEEP MOVING TOWARDS YOUR DREAM.

HOW TO **SET GOALS** SO THAT YOU KNOW YOU ARE MAKING PROGRESS AND CAN FEEL A SENSE OF ACHIEVEMENT.

1. WORK OUT YOUR METHOD

Depending on how old you are, *method* is a word you might have come across in science lessons.

I was rubbish at school, but even I know that method is the bit that explains how a scientist does their experiment: the way they set it up, the process they go through and how they measure the results.

I believe that every dream also requires a method – a way of doing things that you can keep doing and keep getting better at. If the dream is the big thing you are trying to achieve, then the method is the **PROCESS** for how you're going to do it.

People doing almost anything you could imagine have a basic method that allows them to succeed.

Olympic sprinters have a method that is mainly focused on training. They find the best coach they can, they train their bodies and their minds, and they trust that this will help them to be ready when the starting pistol fires at the beginning of the big race.

Fashion brands have a method which is about trying to make clothes that people will want to wear and recommend to their friends. They work with designers who can create trends before they happen.

Window cleaners have a method that is based on being visible to potential customers. If someone in a house with dirty windows sees their neighbour's windows being cleaned, they will probably choose to hire the same window cleaners.

The thing about these methods is that they are **REPEATABLE**. If you keep doing them, then you are likely to succeed.

That's why I say that you need to find a method that can power your dream.

Whatever you are trying to do, you have to know *how* you are going to do it. What is your formula? What is the repeatable process? What are the steps involved?

This doesn't have to be complicated or scientific.

It just has to be something that you keep doing to get results, which moves you closer to your dream.

To work out your method, let's take a step back.

Whatever your dream may be, it puts you in a particular kind of business.

If you are making something like art or custom T-shirts, then you are creating a product and your **BUSINESS** is to sell it.

If you are running a club at school or a social-media channel online, then you are trying to build an audience, and your **BUSINESS** is to get people to sign up and become members or subscribers.

If you are trying to be a performer of some kind, like a DJ or part of a band, then you are trying to get discovered, and your **BUSINESS** is to find people or venues who will give you a chance to play.

First you have to work out: what kind of business am I in (**WHAT** you are doing to achieve your dream)?

Am I trying to sell something to customers? To persuade people to get involved as members of a club or subscribers to a channel? To develop a particular talent or skill?

Once you've worked out the business you are in, then you can think about the method for achieving that (**HOW** you will do it).

I'll use myself as an example.

As an influencer, my **BUSINESS** is to grow my online community and get as many people as possible to engage with the content I create.

My **METHOD** is to find the most interesting, exciting and relatable stories to make videos about. With my team, I try to work out the content that people will really want to watch and which will make them want to subscribe to my channels and be part of my community.

That all helps me to achieve my **DREAM** of helping ten million people – because the bigger my community is, the more I can reach people who need help and connect them to people who can provide it.

For another example, let's look at Stiven, who you met earlier. His **DREAM** is to create a famous hat brand so he can support single parents like his mum.

His **BUSINESS** is selling the hats that he makes.

And his **METHOD** is to create special editions of his hats where only a small number are available to buy. That means the people who get them have the special feeling of owning something not everyone else can have.

Hopefully by now you're starting to see how these three things work together:

Your **DREAM**: the big thing you are trying to achieve (the place you are trying to get to)

Your **BUSINESS**: the way you are going to reach the dream (the engine in the car that will get you to that place)

Your **METHOD**: the repeatable process for doing that (the petrol you put in the tank of that car – or power, if it's electric!)

Now have a go at naming the business that you are in to achieve your dream, and what your method could be for doing that.

MY DREAM IS . . .

THE BUSINESS I AM IN IS . . .

(HINT: THE THING I AM TRYING TO DO AND THE RESULT I AM TRYING TO GET)

MY METHOD IS . . .

(HINT: THE WAY I AM GOING TO DO THAT)

If you can fill in these boxes and feel confident about your answers, then that is a massive step forward!

Because now you know what you need to do, and keep doing, to move towards your dream.

But you can't just keep doing the same thing over and over again and hoping that you are getting it right. If you want to make progress, then you have to plan for it. Which brings us on to our next topic.

2. SET GOALS

You already have a dream, so you may be wondering: why do I need goals? Haven't I done that part?

But a dream is a particular kind of goal. It's big, fairly far away and impossible to achieve in one go.

Achieving our dreams will take time and involve quite a lot of different stages.

That's why you have to set goals along the way.

Just like if someone puts a massive steak on the plate in front of you, you don't try and put the whole thing in your mouth in one go. You cut it up into bits that are easy to chew.

We need to do the same thing with your dream, breaking it down into smaller pieces. Those are your goals.

Of course we all know that setting goals is the easy part. Completing them isn't so simple.

But here's an important part: the way you set a goal **HELPS TO DECIDE IF YOU WILL ACHIEVE IT OR NOT.**

Let's break it down.

A lot of people think that goals are just things that follow the words **'I WILL'.**

- [ ] I will eat less chocolate and ice cream.
- [ ] I will run a faster parkrun.
- [ ] I will get a high score on my spelling test.

But these aren't really goals. They are hopes. They are things we would *like* to achieve, but without any kind of plan (or method!) for achieving them.

We can fix this by adding some things in. A goal has to be more than a thing we want to achieve. It also needs to include:

- ☐ **Something specific we will DO to make that goal happen**
- ☐ **A TIME FRAME for achieving the goal**
- ☐ **A way to MEASURE whether or not we achieved the goal**

Let's look at the chocolate and ice cream example, two things which are close to my heart, and possibly to yours too.

I know I eat too much of both. I'd like to stop doing that so I can be healthier.

But if my goal is just to 'eat less chocolate' or 'be more healthy' then I am almost certainly going to fail.

Those things are too vague. I haven't given myself a method to achieve them. They are 'rules' that are hard to follow and easy to break.

I need to add more detail to this goal if I'm going to achieve it.

What if I said this?

> MY GOAL IS TO REDUCE THE AMOUNT OF CHOCOLATE I EAT TO ONE SMALL BAR EACH WEEK.

Now this is a proper goal. Because I've said **EXACTLY** what I'm going to do – to cut down to a single bar of chocolate. I've also given myself a time frame, and a way to measure it.

This is a harder rule to break, because if I've already had my bar of chocolate for the week, then I will feel guilty about peeling the wrapper off another. My brain will be nagging away at me, saying, 'What about the goal, Simon? You promised!'

Whereas if the goal was just 'eat less chocolate', I can keep saying to myself 'this is the last one' every time I have some more. There is nothing specific to make me keep my word. I can keep cheating because the goal is so vague.

So remember, if you set a goal it needs to include the **SPECIFIC ACTIONS** you will take and it needs to include a **MEASURE OF TIME**.

Now it's your turn. Why don't we look at the example of getting a better mark in a spelling test. Write that out as a goal, remembering that you need to say *how* you are going to achieve it and *when* you are going to take those steps. (Hint: if you want to get better at something, practice is a good place to start.)

MY GOAL IS . . .

....

....

....

....

....

Well done! Now you've got the hang of how to set goals, let's turn our attention back to your dream.

By this point you know what the dream is and you've defined a method for achieving it.

- Perhaps your dream is to be in a famous band, and your method is to get your band to play as many gigs at school events as you can.

- Maybe your dream is to help solve homelessness, and your method is to raise money to give to charities by washing cars or selling cakes.

- Or your dream could be to run a 5 km race, and your method is to go jogging every week to build up your fitness, then maybe to join a running club so you can get some coaching and improve.

Whatever it is, your dream needs to have a method, which is how you work, and goals, which are the short-term things you are working towards.

Let's take the example of a dreamer I have worked with, nine-year-old DJ Chicken Nugget. The video we made together was watched over nineteen million times on TikTok.

His dream? Well that bit is pretty obvious: he wants to be a DJ!

To do that, his *method* has to be to get as many chances as he can, both to improve his skills and to perform.

What goals might he set to help him do that?

One goal might be: *Every week for a month, I will approach someone new who can help me to learn and improve as a DJ.*

This is turning the list we talked about earlier into a goal. For four weeks in a row, Chicken Nugget might contact someone on his list and ask for their help (remember: get a parent or responsible adult to do this with you). Even if only one of those people responds positively, that equals huge progress!

Notice how this goal is *specific* and *time-limited*, as we discussed earlier. It says exactly what to do and in what time frame. The goal leads to a specific action, and you can measure your progress as you go. If it helps, make yourself a list and tick them off one by one.

Now it's your turn. Thinking about DJ Chicken Nugget and everything we've said about goals, why don't you set him a goal to help him with his dream to become a DJ?

A GOOD GOAL FOR DJ CHICKEN NUGGET WOULD BE . . .

....

....

....

....

Good job! Now it's time to come back to **YOUR** dream.

You can guess the next part, can't you?

That's right: it's time for you to set some goals of your own!

This is when we really start to make the dream happen. These are the things you're going to be doing over the next weeks and months that will bring you closer to your dream.

Make sure to include a specific action within each goal and to say when or how often you will take that action.

You don't need to tackle all these goals at once. Some of them might be linked, where progress with one goal helps you to move on to another. If you're creating a product to sell, you could have a goal about creating your product, another about testing it with people who might be interested in it, and a third one about selling it. Or it may be possible to work on all your goals at once.

Right, it's over to you. Your goals are really important: this is your action plan for what happens next, so take your time!

MY FIRST GOAL IS . . .

MY SECOND GOAL IS . . .

MY THIRD GOAL IS . . .

OK, at this point you have a lot to do! You've got your dream now, and you've set the goals that will help you to move towards it.

Once again, my advice is to put the book down. You have my permission to stop reading (for now).

Instead, I want you to start working on your goals! If you've written the goals carefully, then they will contain the actions you need to do to make them happen.

You might just want to focus on the first of your goals, or it may be helpful to try and work on all three together.

However you do it, I want you to try and do **THREE THINGS** before going further with the book. Take three specific actions that help you to achieve a goal. It might be getting some friends to join your club, asking some people for help, finding a customer for your car-washing business or booking a gig for your band.

After each one, come back to the book and tell me how it went. Fill out the boxes opposite to say what you did, what the outcome was, what you learned and what you can do next.

Do this **THREE TIMES** before moving on to the next chapter. If you do one thing, it might not work. But if you try three things, it's very likely that one of them will. After you've done these three things, I'm almost sure that you will have achieved something important and learned a lot.

So have a go, tell me how you're getting on, and I'll see you in the next chapter!

AFTER ACTION ONE

WHAT DID I DO?

WHAT WAS THE RESULT?

WHAT DID I LEARN?

WHAT CAN I DO NEXT?

AFTER ACTION TWO

WHAT DID I DO?

WHAT WAS THE RESULT?

WHAT DID I LEARN?

WHAT CAN I DO NEXT?

AFTER ACTION THREE

WHAT DID I DO?

WHAT WAS THE RESULT?

WHAT DID I LEARN?

WHAT CAN I DO NEXT?

OK!

Chapter 6

I'M STUCK! WHAT SHOULD I DO?

By this point in the journey, you might be flying towards your dream.

Perhaps you've got loads of people signing up for your club or subscribing to your channel. There's a queue of orders for your T-shirts. You've flown through your band or choir audition.

Or perhaps it isn't. Maybe most of the people you've asked for help have ignored you. It's been hard to find customers for your business. You've launched a channel and created content but not many people have watched it.

If you're in the first group, well done. But my advice is: don't take it for granted. Don't expect that it will always be like this.

And if you're in the second group, then my advice is: **DON'T WORRY**. Don't expect that it will always be like this.

One of the few advantages of being my age rather than yours is that I've seen a lot. I know that good times don't always last and bad ones aren't forever.

No one stays in either of these two groups permanently. The people who are doing brilliantly are going to struggle at some point. And the people who are struggling will start doing brilliantly.

That's why I want to take some time to discuss what to do when things go wrong. And why, despite what you think, **THIS CAN ACTUALLY BE A GOOD THING.**

If you've followed my steps above, you may already have had some struggles with your dream. And if you haven't, I promise that you will eventually. Overcoming these is a vital part of making any dream happen. So buckle up, and let's talk about what to do when things don't go to plan.

FAILURE IS OK

I PROMISE!

Shall we talk about why I hated school?

Mostly it's that I wasn't very good at it. Like I told you earlier, my dyslexia wasn't understood and people made fun of my struggles to read. I hope things are different at school now, but if you ever experience something like this, do me a favour and please tell a teacher or a trusted grown-up.

There was also something deeper about the school system I disliked, which I think is still a problem today.

It was the idea that everything came down to a test that you'd either pass or fail.

It said that if you failed the test then you must be an idiot. It meant you hadn't worked hard enough or you weren't clever enough. You were supposed to feel ashamed of getting a low mark.

Now, you may like school and you probably have some brilliant teachers. I don't want to turn you against school (although if you're having a hard time, then I understand and I'm with you).

But I **DO** want to challenge this idea that failure is automatically something bad.

Because while it might be relevant for maths tests, it doesn't apply to real life.

Of course we all *want* to succeed all the time. We want things to go our way. We want to do well.

But it's never going to work every single time. Even the most successful people on Earth fail. Harry Kane misses penalties in big games. Olivia Rodrigo misses high notes on big stages. And if it can happen to them, then it will definitely happen to the rest of us.

The question isn't *if* you will experience failure. It's *when*. And more importantly, **WHAT YOU DO NEXT**.

How do you feel?

How do you respond?

When something goes wrong, our first instinct is usually to feel sad, angry or frustrated. It's a natural response, but it's also a problem if you get stuck there. If you accept that the failure is the end.

In fact, failure is more like the middle of the story, and it leaves us with some important questions.

- DO I GIVE UP OR DO I CARRY ON?
- DO I BLAME MYSELF OR DO I LEARN FROM WHAT HAPPENED?
- DO I EMBRACE NEGATIVE THOUGHTS OR SEEK POSITIVE ONES?

Let's say your dream is to be a fitness influencer and one of your goals is to complete your first 5 km race.

You've started going to junior parkrun, which is almost half that distance. You're going jogging. You've got the right pair of trainers.

But it's not working. You're struggling to get through a 2 km run. Your times aren't improving. You can't see how you're *ever* going to hit that 5 km target.

In theory, you're failing. But are you?

It all depends on what you do next.

This is only a failure **IF YOU LET IT BECOME ONE**.

If you accept failure and don't do anything at all to try and change it.

If you say:

The way to avoid falling into this trap is to turn this 'failure' into something good.

You do that by working out what went wrong. Maybe you need a bit of coaching to improve how you run. Maybe you need more time to build up your fitness. Maybe you need to train your mind a little, thinking about how good it will feel to cross the finish line rather than how tired you are halfway through the race.

This is what 'failure' really is.

IT'S A CHANCE TO WORK OUT WHAT IS GOING WRONG AND HOW TO FIX IT.

To get better at what we're doing.

To make sure we're doing the **RIGHT THINGS** to achieve our dreams.

If you've always thought of failure as a terrible thing, then this is going to sound like weird advice.

That's exactly why we need to think about failure differently.

We need to stop blaming ourselves when things go wrong.

And we need to start accepting that failure is a message. It says try again. Try something different. Learn and improve from this, and you will get better. Then the next time, you won't fail at all.

I know this because, although I've had my fair share of success in life, I have learned most from the times when I failed. Sometimes those failures felt **DISASTROUS**, and I lost millions of pounds on businesses that went wrong. But I became better as a result. I succeeded because I didn't make the same mistakes again. Failure taught me things that I could never have learned any other way.

This is such an important part of any dream.

Of all the things you try – those actions we wrote out in the last chapter, or the list of people we made to contact – not all of them will succeed. In fact, it's possible that **MOST OF THEM** will fail. We won't immediately get what we want. We'll have to try again, to change our approach, or to practise our skills some more.

You have to be prepared for these setbacks and ready to respond with a positive mindset.

One that says:

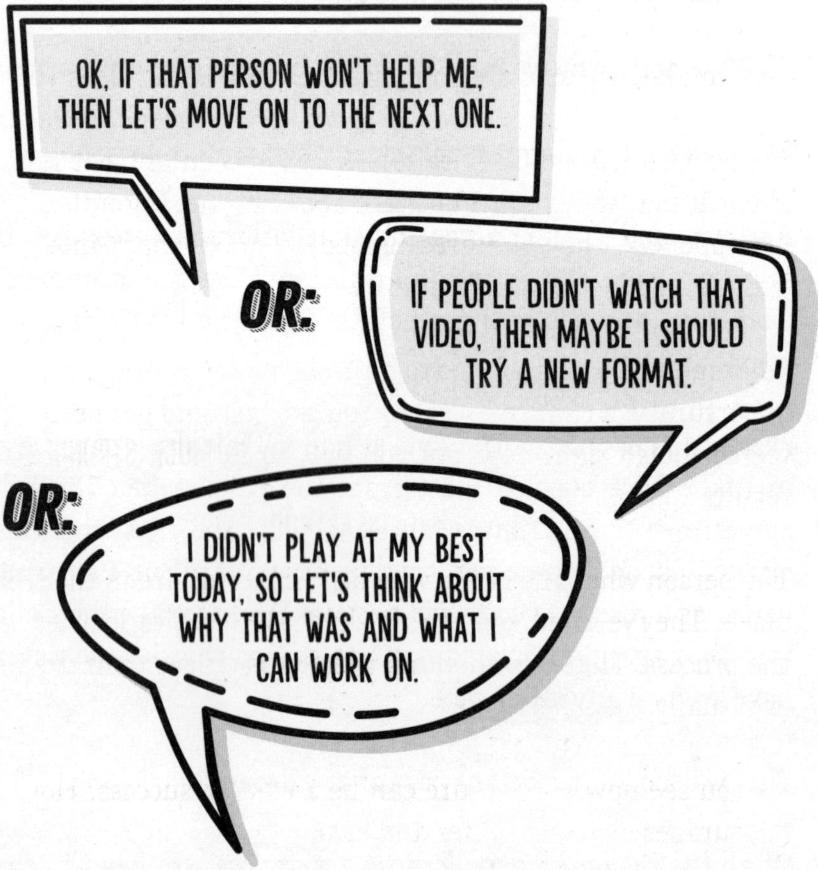

If you go through this process, thinking through the failure rather than letting it overwhelm you, then I promise that you will grow as a person. You will do better the next time. Eventually, you will succeed where you didn't before.

If you've done that, then you never really failed. It was all part of you learning, developing and growing as a person. In my opinion, *that is exactly what success looks like.*

If you're still not convinced, then it might help to flip this around. What about people who always seem to succeed?

That makes them clever, talented and brilliant, doesn't it? Maybe. But let me tell you a secret about people who are always succeeding. They failed. A lot. You might not know about it and they might not talk about it, but I promise you it happened. Those failures helped to make them into the successful people that you admire.

So remember that if you're failing at something, it's an opportunity: a chance to learn. You are going to get better. It feels rubbish right now, but you will be **SO MUCH STRONGER** as result.

The person who fails is one who has risked failure in the first place. They've tried something difficult. They've learned in the process. That sets them up better to achieve their dream eventually.

Do you see now how failure can be a part of success? How it encourages us to get better and keep going?

I hope so. But let's put it to a test (one that you can't pass or fail!).

I want you to think about everything I've just said and work out *three reasons* why failure can be a good thing, and how it can help us with our dreams.

1

FAILURE CAN BE HELPFUL BECAUSE . . .

2

FAILURE CAN BE HELPFUL BECAUSE . . .

3

FAILURE CAN BE HELPFUL BECAUSE . . .

OK, now let's reflect on a time in your life when something happened that might have felt like a failure at the time.

ONE TIME I FELT LIKE I HAD FAILED WAS . . .

BUT LOOKING BACK, ONE LESSON I LEARNED AS A RESULT WAS . . .

We've now learned something important about failure and how to respond to it. As you do that, you will start to develop what I think is the **KEY ABILITY** for achieving your dreams. What is it? Read on to find out.

THE TOP SECRET SKILL

What do you think is the number-one most important skill for being successful and achieving your dream?

- **IS IT BEING CLEVER?**
- **FUNNY?**
- **GOOD AT MATHS?**
- **GOOD AT PUBLIC SPEAKING?**

Well, I have known a lot of brilliant people and studied how they succeeded. None of those things are at the top of my list, though they're all nice to have.

The number-one skill for success in my book is something quite special.

Because **ANYONE** can get good at it. It doesn't matter whether you're tall or not, if you wear glasses, if you're better with words or numbers, or if you prefer cakes or biscuits.

This is a skill that every single person in the world can possess. It's open to all of us. But you have to choose it.

That skill is *perseverance*: the ability to keep going, to overcome obstacles and to adapt as you go.

Why do I think this is the most important thing?

Because it's an almost unbreakable rule that people who persevere get what they want, and the people who fail to persevere don't.

A lot of people are wrong about this. They think talent and ideas are the main ingredients of success.

They're wrong. ✗

If I could hire the most talented person in the world or the most determined person, then it would be the second one every single time. Because I know that the person who perseveres will find a way to win. They will keep trying and they will adjust their approach. They will get better at the things they can't do. They will succeed *because* they persevered.

I promise you that **EVERY SINGLE PERSON YOU ADMIRE** has succeeded because of perseverance.

The best sportspeople had to work and work at their skills from an early age and fight to get a chance to show how good they were.

The best entrepreneurs started businesses that went bust before launching the one that made them millions.

The best actors auditioned for loads of parts they didn't get before getting the one that made their name.

The best content creators had lots of videos that no one ever saw, before hitting on something that made them a success.

The truth is that a lot of people have talent. A lot of people have good ideas. A lot of people have dreams.

Those things are worth relatively little unless you have the desire to keep going. To persevere when it is difficult, knowing that you will get through the tough moments and achieve your dream.

Perseverance means you don't let failure stop you.

You don't give up when things get hard.

You don't let other people talk you out of something you believe in.

I am making a big deal about this because, as you work towards your dream, you are going to have difficult moments.

What if someone says no?

What if they say it's a stupid idea?

What if they laugh at you?

I won't lie to you. Bits of this will be hard. You will try things that don't work. Sometimes it will be difficult and frustrating. A dream is a wonderful thing but it can also be difficult and frustrating when it feels like you're not making progress.

WHEN FACED WITH THESE MOMENTS,

YOU WILL NEED TO SHOW PERSEVERANCE.

You'll have to remind yourself that it's normal to experience setbacks.

That it doesn't mean there's anything wrong with you or your dream.

That you need to keep going, or to find another way to achieve the next goal.

I think perseverance is a bit like a muscle. The more you use it, the stronger it gets. Each time you overcome a problem through perseverance, it will get a little easier to keep going. To deal with the next problem and the one after that.

Now it's over to you. Have a think about a situation where you might need to show perseverance while working towards your dream. Or if it's already happened, then tell me about that!

A SITUATION WHERE I SHOWED PERSEVERANCE IN THE PAST IS . . .

____

____

____

A SITUATION WHERE I MAY NEED TO PERSEVERE IS . . .

____

____

____

If you're at all worried about this, then remember you have one big advantage in all this.

You have a dream! Something that's grounded in your biggest passion, which contains a purpose, and allows you to do something you're good at.

One of the best things about having a dream is it means we know exactly **WHAT** we're trying to do and exactly **WHY** we're trying to do it.

As we work through our goals, sometimes succeeding and sometimes failing, the dream stays with us. It helps us to persevere, because we know everything we're doing is helping us to move towards our end goal. Our dreams are the best reason to keep going.

THERE'S ANOTHER THING TOO. ANOTHER REASON TO PUT PERSEVERANCE AT THE TOP OF YOUR LIST. WHEN YOU DO PERSEVERE, SOMETHING HAPPENS. IT'S SOMETHING BRILLIANT. YOU GET LUCKY.

Despite what you may think, 'luck' isn't something that happens by chance. In my experience, there aren't lucky and unlucky people in the world. There are people who keep trying and people who don't. The ones who don't end up feeling unlucky. And the ones who do *get lucky*.

That's not magic – in fact, it's pretty obvious when you stop to think about it.

Whatever you're trying to do, you have to ask a lot of people to get a few positive responses. The more people you ask, the better chance you have of getting lucky and having someone say yes. Just like the striker who takes more shots is going to score more goals. That's not a lucky player, but one who has tried harder and persevered more.

That's why perseverance is one of the most important skills in life. If you learn to be rational about failure and to keep moving forward, then you're going to get lucky breaks. People will start saying yes when you feared they might say no. Those subscriber and viewer numbers are going to start climbing. You'll make a sale and then another one straight after. Your dream is going to be several steps closer because you showed perseverance and you made your own luck.

That's why I call it the number-one skill for achieving your dream. The good news is it's a skill you can start learning and working on today!

Chapter 7

I'M DOING IT! AM I THERE YET?

By this point, I'm guessing you have been working on your dream for a little while. If you've followed the steps so far, then you have probably done quite a lot!

Now it's time for a stock check: to see how you're doing and what should happen next.

First, I'd like you to tell me a bit about how you've been getting on.

I want you to think about two things here:

THINGS YOU HAVE DONE

These are the actions you have taken, like designing a product, training in your skill, creating content or making art. List these out so you can see how much work you've put in!

THINGS YOU HAVE ACHIEVED

These are the results you have accomplished by taking the actions you just listed – like getting a hundred people to subscribe to your channel, finding three customers for your business, or getting your first part in a school play.

ONE THING I'VE *DONE* IS . . .

A SECOND THING I'VE *DONE* IS . . .

A THIRD THING I'VE *DONE* IS . . .

ONE THING I'VE *ACHIEVED* IS . . .

A SECOND THING I'VE *ACHIEVED* IS . . .

A THIRD THING I'VE *ACHIEVED* IS . . .

Before we go any further, I want to say:

I hope writing out those answers reminds you just how much you've already achieved! Remember that lots of people never even get started with their dreams. You should be very proud of yourself for getting this far.

But I know you're not going to sit back and be satisfied with having crossed a few goals off your list. You want to know: what's next? How can I go further? When will I actually achieve the dream?

I think this is a good point in the journey to stop and reflect. By this stage, you've done enough to judge how well you are doing. Is what you're doing working? Are you enjoying it? Are you keen to do more?

You've already told me what you've done towards your dream and what you've achieved. Now I want you to think a little bit about how you **FEEL**. This is really important too, because our dreams are meant to be fulfilling. It should be fun!

THE THING I'VE MOST ENJOYED SO FAR IS . . .

....

....

....

THE THING I'VE FOUND MOST DIFFICULT SO FAR IS . . .

....

....

....

OK, we're starting to build a picture about how you're getting on with your dream. You've now thought about what you have achieved, what you've enjoyed most while working towards your dream and what you've found difficult.

Now for one more question. The big one. **IS IT WORKING?** Are you making progress towards your dream?

Note that I say *progress towards*. Because **I DON'T EXPECT** you to have achieved your dream by this point. You might have taken some brilliant strides. But a dream is a journey and it can take a long time to get there. I don't want you to worry if you feel like you've only gone a little bit of the way – that's completely normal. I'm over 50 years old and I am still working on my dream!

Instead of worrying about completing your dream, I want you to think about the progress you've made since the start of this book.

What do I mean by **PROGRESS?**

It's something that brings you *closer* to your dream. Something that creates momentum, where you are moving forward and each step naturally leads on to the next one. Progress is when you think: *Now I've done this, it allows me to do that.*

If your dream is to become an influencer, then progress is having a channel with some subscribers, which you can continue to grow. One hundred followers become two hundred, and so on.

If your dream is to run a marathon or climb a mountain, then progress is being able to run further or climb higher than you could at the beginning, encouraging you to keep improving and setting new personal bests.

If your dream is to be a performer of any kind, like a DJ or in a band, then progress is having done a few gigs, which helps you to get more because now people know you can do it.

Progress can also be how you *feel* about your dream. Are you more confident in your ability? Have you proven to yourself that you can do something that you were afraid of doing? Do you believe more in what you are trying to do?

Now it's your turn. I'd like you to think hard about everything you've done so far and give me **THREE WAYS** in which you have made progress since we started this journey. Remember to include details because that will help your brain remember the progress you've made!

THE FIRST WAY I'VE MADE PROGRESS TOWARDS MY DREAM IS . . .

THE SECOND WAY I'VE MADE PROGRESS TOWARDS MY DREAM IS . . .

THE THIRD WAY I'VE MADE PROGRESS TOWARDS MY DREAM IS . . .

Hopefully that's been a useful reminder of how far you've come since we started on this journey!

Now we've done some looking back, let's look forward and focus on what's next.

What should you do now?

The answer to that depends on a few things.

ARE YOU HAPPY WITH THE PROGRESS YOU'VE MADE SO FAR?

ARE YOU HAVING FUN WORKING ON YOUR DREAM?

ARE YOU EXCITED ABOUT TAKING THE NEXT STEPS?

To work out what you should do, I'd like you to give yourself a mark out of 10 on each of those three things, where 10 is the most happy and excited, and 1 is the least.

How happy are you with your progress so far?

○ ○ ○ ○ ○ ○ ○ ○ ○ ○

1 2 3 4 5 6 7 8 9 10

How much fun are you having?

○ ○ ○ ○ ○ ○ ○ ○ ○ ○

1 2 3 4 5 6 7 8 9 10

How excited are you to do more?

○ ○ ○ ○ ○ ○ ○ ○ ○ ○

1 2 3 4 5 6 7 8 9 10

At this point, I've got some options for you. Depending on how you're feeling and the scores you've just given yourself, there are some different paths you can take. Let's go through them.

OPTION 1: KEEP GOING

The right option if you scored yourself 7 or above on the questions we've just done.

If everything is going pretty well, you're feeling happy about what you've achieved and excited about what comes next, then this is the one for you. The advice is really simple: you should carry on!

Whatever you're doing is working, so the best thing is to do more of it! Keep creating those videos, going to those training sessions, baking those cakes and washing those cars. Be happy that you're moving towards your dream and feeling good about it.

My challenge to you at this point is: what else could you be doing? Can you try something new that will add to what you're already working on? Is there a new design technique you could work on for your T-shirt brand? A different kind of training you could be doing? An alternative video format for your channel?

Keep looking for ways to improve and move towards your dream. Try things out and see how you go! You can always go back to earlier chapters and repeat the exercises to remind yourself how to come up with plans and set goals.

OPTION 2: CHANGE DIRECTION

The right option if you scored yourself 4–6 on the questions we've just done.

You're somewhere in the middle: it could be better, and it could be worse.

That means you probably need to make some changes, but nothing drastic. I don't want you ripping out pages of the book and throwing them in the bin!

Think of it a bit like one of those long car journeys you've probably had on holiday. The driver has taken a wrong turn, you've gone the wrong way for a few miles and everyone is starting to get a bit hot and bothered.

It's time to take a deep breath and to have a close look at the map. Because although you've gone a bit off course, it doesn't take much to get back on track. Soon you'll be sitting in a comfortable chair, in the sun, sipping a cold drink.

Your dream is not so different from that long drive. You might start out knowing where you're going, but it's easy to get lost. My guess is that you probably have the **RIGHT DREAM**, but you need to think a bit more about your method and goals. Go back to Chapter 5 and have a look at the exercises. Get a piece of paper and do them again.

Remember that you know things you didn't when you tried this the first time. You've learned a lot about your dream and yourself. Your answers are probably going to be better now. So redo the exercises, compare the before and after, and come up with a new plan of attack for your dream.

OPTION 3: START AGAIN

The right option if you scored yourself 1–3 on the questions we've just done.

OK, you've given yourself a really low set of scores. The first thing I want to say is: don't panic!

We need to find out the reason why this isn't working for you and then we need to fix it.

First, I'd like you to ask yourself why you feel unhappy with your progress, or why you're not having fun.

If you can work out **WHY** this isn't as interesting or exciting as you'd hoped, then you may be able to make some changes to what you're doing.

It's also possible that you need to make a bigger change, and that you should start again, going back to Chapter 2 and doing the exercises again.

That probably sounds like a complete disaster, and makes you feel like we've wasted all the work so far.

But it's not!

Shall I let you in on a secret?

Sometimes the **BEST THING** you can do is hold up your hands and accept that you were wrong. It takes a strong person to decide that what they're doing isn't working. A lot of people just carry on, hoping that something magical will happen.

But it won't. To change how you feel about something, you have to change what you're doing and how you're doing it. Which means that if your dream *isn't* making you happy or excited, *it might not actually be your dream after all.*

If this is where you are, don't feel bad about it. Don't be cross with yourself for having 'got it wrong'.

Remember what we just discussed about failure. It's not the end of the game, it's a turning point. Even if you don't like how things have gone so far, you have learned a lot about yourself and how to get things done that you didn't know before.

You're in a **MUCH BETTER POSITION NOW** to think about and work towards your dream than you were when you first opened this book. So you're not really starting again. You're not losing all your progress. You have come such a long way, even if you're having to start with a fresh sheet of paper.

If you still don't believe me, then maybe take inspiration from some of the most famous businesses in the world. I could fill another book with examples of companies that had to make major changes before they started succeeding.

If you've ever chewed a piece of gum, you might like to know that the biggest maker of it in the world, Wrigley, started out as a company making soap and baking powder (two things you definitely don't want to put in your mouth!). In fact, they used to give away packs of gum *for free*, until they realized it was the product people really wanted and began selling it.

Or if you've ever owned a Nintendo Switch or played a game on one, consider that the company behind it has existed since 1889. For most of its history it made playing cards, not games consoles.

And I'm pretty sure that you've spent at least a bit of time on YouTube. The people who started that company thought it would be a dating website. They had no idea what video sharing and content creation would become.

I've given you those examples to show that **AMAZING THINGS** can happen from changing course. The path you start on isn't the one that you have to stick to. Success often comes when things go wrong and we adjust to try something new, using everything we've learned to make better choices.

That's why I don't want you to feel down if you end up starting again. Because I'm confident that you will get it right this time. Thanks to everything you've learned so far, you'll be racing towards your dream twice as fast!

In fact, I'm so confident that I bet once you have been through this process again, you will be grateful that you failed the first time. Go back to Chapter 6 and think about times you might have failed in the past, which now don't feel as painful as they did at the time. Because that failure will have taught you so much. It will have shown you what it takes to succeed. And this time you will.

Chapter 8

I'VE FINISHED! WHAT DID I LEARN?

We're coming towards the end of our journey together.

So, what have you learned? And what should you do next?

I want to leave you with three lessons summing up everything we've covered. If you take any ideas away from reading this book, these are the ones to remember.

LESSON 1: YOU CAN DO IT!

The most important lesson is the most simple one, but for some people the most difficult to understand.

YOU CAN DO THINGS. Most of the time, doing something beats thinking about it. Actions are more important than words.

When you spend too much time thinking or trying to predict what will happen, it **GETS HARDER** to act. Your brain comes up with all sorts of reasons for delaying action or doing nothing. The longer we spend waiting or preparing to do something, the more difficult it becomes to actually do it.

I hope by now you've learned that nothing is stopping you from chasing your dreams – right now. You don't need to ask permission and you shouldn't wait for someone to tell you it's the right time to start.

You can make the first designs and products for your fashion brand.

You can record and upload the first piece of content to your channel.

You can design the first version of your app (the AI tools are so good now that even I could do this!).

Despite this, our first instinct is often **NOT** to take action. It's to give a reason why we can't do something.

We might say that we're busy.

Or that it's too hard.

Or that we don't have the knowledge or experience.

But these things are excuses. They are reasons we come up with to avoid taking action.

We have to ignore the inner voice saying that we shouldn't and we can't.

And we have to tell ourselves: **COME ON! WE CAN DO IT!**

It's hard to overcome these doubts, but when we do, something amazing happens.

WHEN YOU TAKE ACTION, *IT LEADS TO MORE ACTION.*

Once you've created one product or video, or you've found one customer or subscriber, then you **WANT** to find the next one. Your brain flips from telling you not to do it to encouraging you to do it again. You realize how much fun it is to see your dream starting to become a reality. And you're suddenly eager to tackle the next thing. That is the magic of taking action. Of believing in your ability to do things.

If you put this book down for the last time understanding that the ball is in your court and your dream is in *your* control, then I have done my job. That is a lesson you can carry with you all through your life.

Because the person who takes responsibility, and who doesn't wait to be told what to do, is someone who controls their own destiny. Eventually, they are going to achieve their dream.

LESSON 2: ASK FOR HELP

While it's true that you need to take responsibility for your dream, that doesn't mean you're on your own.

In fact, the opposite is true.

There has probably never been more help available, in more different ways.

There are YouTube tutorials about everything you could think of.

There are AI chatbots that can answer every question you could think of asking (don't assume they're always right, but it's a good place to start).

And of course you have your grown-ups, siblings, friends and family, who have a huge role to play in your dream.

It would be silly not to use all the help that's out there.

You will need it to make progress with your dream.

Because no one has ever succeeded on their own. *Everyone* needed help.

You might need help to work out how to do something you've never tried before – like creating the thumbnail on a YouTube video, or getting your design printed on to a T-shirt.

You might need help to deal with a problem you're stuck on – like trying to find customers for your business or subscribers for your channel.

You might need help to improve your skills as an athlete, musician or DJ.

I believe in asking for help. In fact, I believe in it so much that I started an entire business so that people can get help with their businesses (it's called HelpBnk).

Help is a complicated thing. Some people think they should do everything themselves. They worry about asking for help. What if the other person says no? What if they say your dream is a terrible idea? What if they laugh at you?

Those things could happen (and it wouldn't be the end of the world if they did). But in my experience, it's much more likely that people *will* help you.

Here's another secret: most people like being asked for help. They like giving advice, sharing their experience, and doing something good for another person.

You may be surprised by how many people are willing to help you with your dream.

But first you have to ask for their help. Ask people what they think about your dream and if they have any advice. Ask them to show you how to do things. Ask them how you can get better.

You will need this help to make progress towards your dream.

So get used to admitting what you don't know and asking for help.

Because the really smart people aren't the ones who know everything. They're the people who ask for help.

LESSON 3: HAVE FUN

If you follow the two lessons above, getting used to taking action and asking for help, then you're on the right track.

You're going to make a lot of progress towards your dream just by doing those two things.

But that's not quite all. There's one more thing I'd like you to remember as you finish the book.

It takes us back to one of the first things we discussed.

Remember the three ingredients of a dream?

The first and most important of those was **PASSION**.

A dream is built from passion: it's inspired by the things and people you most care about.

If you like, underline that sentence. It might be the most important one in the entire book.

The whole point of having a dream is that it allows you to do something you love.

I want you to learn this now, because as you get older, doing things you love gets harder.

You'll be told that your hobbies are less important than passing exams.

That work should take priority over play.

That you should squeeze the things you enjoy doing into little bits of spare time.

Having a dream is the best way to avoid that trap. It allows you to do what you enjoy and to see if you can turn it into more than a hobby.

Eventually, it might become a proper business, allowing you to turn your passion into a career.

You don't need to worry about that just yet, but I do want you to hold on to the idea of having fun and doing things you love.

Far too many of the grown-ups I meet have forgotten this. They think they're **NOT ALLOWED** to chase their dreams, or that they need to wait until they've made money by working in a job they hate. They've listened to so many stories about the importance of getting a job and buying a house that they've lost sight of the most important things – living a life with purpose and following their passions.

Those passions will be different for each of us. Some of us like gardening and some prefer gaming. Your thing might be making music or skateboarding. It could be something completely different that I haven't even mentioned yet.

Whatever it is, it's *your* passion. The thing that makes you happy, relaxed and excited. Why wouldn't you want to do more of it?

THAT'S EXACTLY WHAT A DREAM IS ABOUT. SPENDING MORE TIME DOING WHAT WE LOVE AND USING THAT PASSION TO FUEL A BIGGER PURPOSE.

It's really important you don't forget this as you move forward with your dream. There will be difficult moments and things that definitely aren't enjoyable. Through all that, you have to keep reminding yourself that it's meant to be fun. That you're doing this thing because you love to do it. That it's your passion.

Knowing this will help to carry you through the tough days. It will remind you that something good is always around the corner. That your dream is always with you.

Those are my lessons. But this is *your* book: by now, you have written almost as much in its pages as I have!

Now I want to turn the tables and ask what **YOU** have learned from the book.

Imagine that you were talking to a friend who hasn't read this. What would you say to them? What advice would you give about how to get started? What are your top tips, based on everything you've read in here and done towards your dream?

I want you to write out three **BIG LESSONS** from the book in your own words. As you do this exercise, try to think about the things you've found most interesting, difficult, exciting or surprising. The moments that evoke strong emotions in us are usually the ones when we are learning something important.

THE FIRST BIG THING I'VE LEARNED IS . . .

....

....

....

THE SECOND BIG THING I'VE LEARNED IS . . .

....

....

....

THE THIRD BIG THING I'VE LEARNED IS . . .

....

....

....

ONE LAST THING: HELP SOMEONE ELSE

OK, we've done my lessons and yours.

Before we finish, I have one thing left to say.

So far we've talked a lot about you, your dream and what other people can do to help you.

The final thing you need to do is flip the whole thing around.

This may sound strange, but I want you to stop thinking about your dream for a moment.

Instead let's talk about other people.

Because if you can have a dream, then so can everyone else you know. Your siblings. Your friends at school or in your home education group. The other kids who live on your road.

Their dreams are just as important and interesting as yours is.

Why does that matter to you?

Partly it's about being a good person and caring about the other people in our lives.

It's also more than that. This is something it took me a long time to find out, and I think it's one of the most important things I've ever learned.

WHEN WE HELP OTHER PEOPLE, WE ARE ALSO HELPING OURSELVES.

Helping is a bit like magic: it unlocks a part of our brain that we otherwise can't access. When you make an effort to help other people with *their dreams*, it helps you with yours too.

Why is that? I think there are a few reasons:

- Helping other people chase their dreams gives us a new perspective: we see people tackling similar challenges to our own, and we learn from them.

- When we listen to other people's ideas and tell them what we think, it encourages us to share what we've found out from pursuing our dreams. That helps to remind us of everything we've learned.

- Being the person who *gives help* allows us to understand the point of view of the people *we* are asking for help.

As you can see, there are good and rational reasons for helping your friends with their dreams, but I don't want you to worry too much about them. I just want you to trust that helping other people is a good thing. I promise that it will make you feel good and that it will help you with your own dream.

I know that I have learned more from helping people with their dreams in the last five years than I did in the previous twenty years of running a business, focused just on what I was doing.

That is the power of being generous and helpful. It allows us to see the world differently and it gives us new ideas.

So the next time your brother or sister, best friend or person you sit next to on the school bus tells you what they are doing, don't ignore them. Don't change the subject to your dream.

Instead, listen to them and ask questions. See if there is anything you can do to help them.

It's one minute out of your day, and I promise it will be time well-spent.

That's my last piece of advice to you.

THE BEST WAY TO WORK ON YOUR DREAM IS TO HELP SOMEONE ELSE WITH THEIRS.

I know that this doesn't sound right.

But all my experience tells me that this is how we grow and make progress.

Once you've tried it, I think you'll agree with me.

So go on: find someone to help. Do it today. And then do it again. Make a habit of helping people.

Your dream will be waiting for you. And you'll be more prepared than ever to take it to the next level.

Chapter 9

THE DREAM DIARY

Our time together is almost up.

I hope you've learned a lot and most of all had a lot of fun thinking about your dream and starting to make it happen.

Although the book may be finishing, the journey towards your dream is not.

Right now I hope you're thinking about what happens next, and which of the options I gave you in Chapter 7 to choose. I bet you've got loads of ideas about how to keep your dream going or get a new idea started!

To help with that, I want to leave you with one last exercise.

I call it the **DREAM DIARY**.

It works like this. Each month for the next six months, I want you to open the book again and note down how you're getting on.

Tell me about what you've been doing, what you've learned and what you're going to do next.

This is really important because we need a way to measure our progress: to pat ourselves on the back for hitting goals and then to set new ones. Keeping a diary helps us to stay focused and to build momentum towards the dream.

It's also really interesting! You get to look back at what you were thinking a week, a month or six months ago. You might think that you know *so much more* now than you did then. I bet you'll be proud of how much you've achieved in that time.

So keep coming back to the diary, filling it out for as long as you find it helpful. If you like, set your own questions and come up with your own format.

Because it's your dream now. You get to tell the story. You get to decide what happens next.

Feel free to tell me about it @SimonSquibb (please ask a grown-up for permission) and ask all the questions that I haven't answered.

Until then, good luck! Be brilliant! And most importantly, keep dreaming!

OK!

_______________'S

DREAM DIARY

MONTH 1

ONE THING I'VE DONE IS . . .

ONE THING I'VE LEARNED IS . . .

ONE THING I WANT TO DO NEXT IS . . .

ONE GOAL I'M SETTING MYSELF IS . . .

MONTH 2

ONE THING I'VE DONE IS . . .

ONE THING I'VE LEARNED IS . . .

ONE THING I WANT TO DO NEXT IS . . .

ONE GOAL I'M SETTING MYSELF IS . . .

MONTH 3

ONE THING I'VE DONE IS . . .

ONE THING I'VE LEARNED IS . . .

ONE THING I WANT TO DO NEXT IS . . .

ONE GOAL I'M SETTING MYSELF IS . . .

MONTH 4

ONE THING I'VE DONE IS . . .

ONE THING I'VE LEARNED IS . . .

ONE THING I WANT TO DO NEXT IS . . .

ONE GOAL I'M SETTING MYSELF IS . . .

MONTH 5

ONE THING I'VE DONE IS . . .

ONE THING I'VE LEARNED IS . . .

ONE THING I WANT TO DO NEXT IS . . .

ONE GOAL I'M SETTING MYSELF IS . . .

MONTH 6

ONE THING I'VE DONE IS . . .

ONE THING I'VE LEARNED IS . . .

ONE THING I WANT TO DO NEXT IS . . .

ONE GOAL I'M SETTING MYSELF IS . . .

ACKNOWLEDGEMENTS

Most importantly I want to thank Helen Griffiths, the best wife and mother in the world, and Aidan, who teaches me more than I could ever teach him.

Thanks to my older brother, Christian, who showed me the world and my potential.

To my partners at HelpBnk, who believe as much as I do in the importance of enabling people to dream.

To Fenella Bates and the team at Puffin, who believed in this book and made it happen.

To Adam Gauntlett, my agent, and to Josh Davis who helped me to write it down.

To all the dreamers young and old who have shared their hopes and fears with me.

And a special thanks to the 'big kids' who work with me every day to make their dreams possible: Adam, Adam, Adrien, Arthur, Azalia, Bella, Ben, Ben, Callum, Chris, Chloe, Clemens, Dudley, Guy, Guy, Jack, James, Joe, Jonny, Katie, Kim, Lucas, Ninos, Ollie, Park, Phebe, Rich, Robin, Samir, Stephen, Thisath, Thomas, Tobias, Tom and Yordi. Together we will help millions help millions more to dream!

Finally to all the many people, in different places and at different points in my life, who helped me and without whom none of this would have happened.